The Economic Enlightenment

Decoding Financial Forces

Eden Wilkinson

Contents

1 Foundations of Economic Thought

Economics, at its core, is the study of how societies manage scarce resources. This fundamental principle of scarcity dictates that resources are limited while human wants are effectively boundless. We cannot have everything we desire; therefore, we must make choices. These choices, both individual and collective, form the basis of economic activity. Understanding how these choices are made and their consequences is the first step toward economic enlightenment. Consider, for example, a government deciding how to allocate its budget. Does it invest in education, infrastructure, or healthcare? Each choice necessitates forgoing other potentially valuable options. This inherent trade-off underscores the importance of careful consideration and prioritization in economic decision-making.

The concept of opportunity cost further refines our understanding of choice. It represents the value of the next best alternative sacrificed when making a decision. It's not simply the monetary cost of an action but the potential benefits forgone by choosing one path over another. A student choosing to attend university incurs not only tuition fees but also forgoes the potential earnings they could have made by entering the workforce directly after high school. Recognizing and evaluating opportunity costs, both explicit and implicit, leads to more informed and rational decision-making. It highlights the true cost of any decision and allows for a more comprehensive assessment of potential benefits.

Visualizing trade-offs and opportunity costs is often achieved through the Production Possibilities Frontier (PPF). This graphical model illustrates the various combinations of goods and services an economy can produce given its limited resources and technology. The PPF demonstrates the concept of efficiency – producing the maximum output possible with available resources. Any point inside the PPF represents inefficiency, meaning the economy is not fully utilizing its potential. Points outside the PPF are unattainable with current resources and technology. The PPF also illustrates the potential for economic growth. Through technological advancements or increases in resources, the PPF can shift outward, expanding the range of possible production combinations. This outward shift represents the ability of an economy to produce more goods and services, satisfying more wants and needs.

Within the constraints of scarcity, different economic systems have emerged to address the fundamental economic problem of resource allocation. Broadly categorized as market, command, and mixed economies, each system adopts a unique approach to production, distribution, and consumption. Market economies rely on decentralized decision-making, with prices determined by the interaction of supply and demand. Command economies, conversely, centralize economic planning, with government authorities dictating production quotas and prices. Mixed economies combine elements of both, balancing market forces with government intervention. Each system presents its own set of advantages and disadvantages, influencing economic efficiency, equity, and individual freedoms. Understanding these differences is crucial for analyzing the diverse economic landscapes across the globe.

Finally, incentives play a critical role in shaping economic behavior. Incentives can be positive, like rewards or bonuses, or negative, like penalties or fines. They influence individual and collective choices, motivating specific actions and discouraging others. Governments use tax policies to incentivize investment, savings, or charitable giving. Businesses utilize performance-based bonuses to motivate employees. Understanding how incentives operate is crucial for predicting and influencing economic outcomes. Designing effective incentive structures can promote desired behaviors and contribute to positive economic outcomes. However, poorly designed incentives can lead to unintended consequences and market distortions, highlighting the importance of careful consideration and analysis. By understanding the interplay of scarcity, opportunity cost, production possibilities, economic systems, and incentives, we lay the foundation for a deeper understanding of the complex forces shaping the economic world. This foundational knowledge empowers us to analyze economic challenges, evaluate policy decisions, and ultimately, make more informed choices in our own economic lives.

1.1 Scarcity and Choice

We live in a world of limited resources. This fundamental truth underpins every economic decision, every trade-off, and every choice we make, whether we consciously acknowledge it or not. From the grand scale of national budgets to the personal dilemma of choosing between a morning coffee and a bus ticket, scarcity shapes our reality. Understanding its influence is crucial to navigating the complexities of our economic lives.

Scarcity isn't just about having too little money. It applies to time, energy, natural resources, even attention spans. Consider a farmer with a limited plot of land. They can't grow everything. They must choose between corn and wheat, potatoes and soybeans. Each decision involves an opportunity cost – the value of the next best alternative forgone. If they choose corn, they lose the potential harvest of wheat. This principle, though simple, is profound. It highlights the inherent trade-offs in every decision, forcing us to prioritize and make difficult choices.

The concept of scarcity is inextricably linked to choice. Without scarcity, there's no need for choice. If resources were infinite, we could have everything we wanted. We wouldn't need to budget our time, prioritize our spending, or strategize about how to allocate resources. But this utopian ideal doesn't reflect the world we inhabit. Instead, we must constantly evaluate our options, weighing the benefits of one choice against the costs of another. This process, while often challenging, is the essence of economic decision-making.

Consider a student deciding how to spend their weekend. They could work extra hours at their part-time job, earning money for tuition. They could dedicate the time to studying, potentially improving their grades. Or they could prioritize social activities, investing in friendships and personal wellbeing. Each option has its own benefits and costs. The student must consider their priorities, their long-term goals, and the relative value they place on each potential outcome.

Prices play a crucial role in managing scarcity. In a market economy, prices act as signals, reflecting the relative scarcity of goods and services. When something is in high demand but limited supply, the price tends to rise. This higher price discourages consumption and encourages production, helping to balance supply and demand. Conversely, when a good is plentiful, the price falls, making it more accessible to consumers.

Think about the price of gasoline. When global oil production decreases, gasoline prices typically rise. This increase encourages consumers to find alternative transportation methods, like carpooling or public transit, reducing demand. Simultaneously, the higher price incentivizes oil companies to explore new sources of oil or invest in alternative energy technologies, increasing supply.

The interplay of scarcity, choice, and price forms the foundation of market dynamics. Understanding these principles allows us to analyze economic trends, predict consumer behavior, and make informed decisions in our own lives. It allows us to appreciate the complexities of resource allocation and the interconnectedness of global markets. It empowers us to navigate the trade-offs we face daily, making choices that align with our values and goals.

Effective resource management becomes crucial in the context of scarcity. Whether on a personal, organizational, or societal level, maximizing the utility of limited resources is essential for achieving desired outcomes. This requires careful planning, prioritization, and a clear understanding of the available options. It necessitates the development of strategies to minimize waste, optimize efficiency, and ensure sustainable practices.

Consider a government allocating its annual budget. It must balance competing demands for funding, from healthcare and education to infrastructure and defense. This involves making difficult choices, prioritizing certain areas over others based on societal needs and available resources. It also requires careful consideration of the long-term implications of these decisions, ensuring that resources are allocated in a sustainable and responsible manner.

The concept of scarcity extends beyond material goods and

services. It applies to intangible resources as well, such as time and attention. In our increasingly fast-paced world, these resources are becoming ever more precious. Learning to manage our time effectively, prioritizing tasks, and minimizing distractions are essential skills for navigating the demands of modern life. It requires setting boundaries, saying no to unnecessary commitments, and focusing our energy on activities that align with our values and goals.

Scarcity and choice are fundamental concepts that shape our economic lives. Understanding these principles empowers us to make informed decisions, manage resources effectively, and navigate the complexities of a world with limited resources. It provides a framework for understanding market dynamics, consumer behavior, and the trade-offs inherent in every choice we make. By recognizing the limitations imposed by scarcity, we can appreciate the value of resources and make choices that maximize our well-being and contribute to a more sustainable future.

1.2 Opportunity Cost

We make choices every single day. From the mundane, like choosing between a bagel and a muffin for breakfast, to the monumental, like deciding on a career path. Each decision, no matter how small, carries with it an unseen weight: the opportunity cost. This represents the value of the next best alternative that we forgo when making a choice. Understanding this concept is crucial for navigating the complexities of personal finance and making sound decisions that align with our long-term goals.

Imagine you have $1,000 to invest. You could put it into a high-yield savings account, potentially earning a modest but steady return. Alternatively, you could invest it in the stock market, hoping for higher returns but accepting the inherent risks involved. Choosing the savings account means forgoing the potential (but uncertain) higher gains from the stock market. Conversely, choosing the stock market means missing out on the guaranteed return, however small, of the savings account. This trade-off, this "what could have been," is the opportunity cost.

Opportunity cost isn't just about money. It applies to time, energy, and even relationships. Think about pursuing a graduate degree. The financial cost is substantial: tuition, fees, and often forgone income. However, there's also a significant time cost. Those years spent studying could have been used to advance your career in your current field, start a family, or travel the world. The opportunity cost of the graduate degree is the combined value of all those experiences you chose not to pursue.

One of the most common financial pitfalls is failing to consider the long-term opportunity cost of small, everyday expenses. That daily latte, the impulsive online purchase, the subscription service you rarely use – individually, they may seem insignificant. However, these small expenditures, compounded over time, can amount to a substantial sum. The money you spend on these seemingly harmless indulgences could be invested, earning returns that could significantly improve your financial future. The opportunity cost of these small expenses is the potential future wealth you're forfeiting.

Effectively evaluating opportunity cost requires careful consideration of your priorities and goals. What truly matters to you? What are you willing to sacrifice to achieve your long-term objectives? If financial security is a top priority, you might be willing to forgo certain luxuries to maximize your savings and investments. If work-life balance is paramount, you might choose a less demanding, lower-paying job over a high-pressure, high-earning career. There's no right or wrong answer; the key is to make conscious, informed decisions that align with your values.

Another crucial aspect of understanding opportunity cost is recognizing that it's not always quantifiable. While the financial cost of a decision is often easily calculated, the intangible costs, such as time, experiences, and relationships, are more difficult to measure. How do you put a price on the joy of spending time with your family or the personal fulfillment of pursuing a passion project? These intangible costs are no less real or important than the financial ones; in fact, they often carry greater weight in the long run.

To effectively incorporate the concept of opportunity cost into your decision-making process, consider the following strategies. First, clearly define your goals. What do you hope to achieve in the short term and the long term? Having a clear vision of your objectives will help you prioritize your choices and make decisions that move you closer to your desired outcomes. Second, identify your alternatives. What are the different options available to you? Brainstorming multiple possibilities allows you to compare and contrast the potential costs and benefits of each choice.

Third, evaluate the potential costs and benefits of each alternative. Consider both the tangible and intangible factors. What are the financial implications of each choice? How will each option impact your time, energy, and relationships? Creating a pros and cons list for each alternative can be a helpful tool in this process. Fourth, choose the option that best aligns with your goals and values. Remember, the best choice isn't always the one with the highest potential financial return. Sometimes, the most valuable option is the one that brings the greatest personal fulfillment or aligns with your overall life priorities.

Finally, regularly review and reassess your decisions. Circumstances change, and what might have been the best choice at one point in time may no longer be the optimal option. Periodically revisiting your decisions allows you to adjust your course as needed and ensure that you remain on track to achieve your goals. By understanding and applying the concept of opportunity cost, you can make more informed decisions, maximize your resources, and ultimately create a more fulfilling and prosperous life. Remember, every choice has a cost. The key is to make choices that align with your values and move you closer to your desired future.

1.3 Production Possibilities

We live in a world of limitations. Time, resources, energy – all finite. Understanding these constraints is fundamental to effective decision-making, particularly in production. Recognizing that we can't have everything forces us to make choices, to prioritize, and to strive for the most efficient use of what we have. This concept, captured by the production possibilities frontier, is a cornerstone of economic thinking.

The production possibilities frontier (PPF) is a model illustrating the various combinations of two goods or services that an economy can produce when all resources are fully and efficiently employed. Imagine a simplified world where a society only produces two things: bread and computers. The PPF would visually represent the different combinations of bread and computers that this society could produce given its limited resources like labor, land, and capital. A point on the curve itself represents maximum efficiency – all resources are being used optimally. Any point inside the curve signifies underutilization – resources are being wasted or not used to their full potential. Points outside the curve are currently unattainable given existing resources and technology.

The shape of the PPF is crucial. It's typically bowed outwards, reflecting the law of increasing opportunity cost. This law states that as you produce more of one good, the opportunity cost of producing an additional unit of that good increases. In our bread and computer example, shifting production from computers to bread initially requires sacrificing relatively few computers. However, as we continue to shift resources towards bread production, the opportunity cost rises. We start to sacrifice increasingly more computers for each additional loaf of bread. This is because resources are not perfectly adaptable between the production of different goods. Some resources are better suited for computer production, while others are more efficient for baking bread.

Consider a skilled programmer. They might be reasonably effective at baking bread, but their true expertise lies in software development. As we shift them from computer programming to bread baking, we lose a significant amount of potential computer output for a relatively small gain in bread production. This increasing opportunity cost is reflected in the bowed-out shape of the PPF. A straight-line PPF would imply constant opportunity cost, which is rarely realistic.

Understanding the PPF allows us to analyze the trade-offs inherent in every production decision. Choosing to produce more of one good necessitates producing less of another. This concept highlights the importance of careful resource allocation. Societies and businesses must constantly evaluate their priorities and make choices that align with their goals. Do they prioritize feeding their population, or investing in technological advancement? The PPF helps visualize these trade-offs and facilitates informed decision-making.

Technological advancements and increases in resource availability can shift the PPF outwards, expanding the range of attainable production possibilities. Innovation in bread-making technology, for instance, might allow for greater bread production with the same amount of resources. Similarly, discovering new sources of raw materials or increasing the labor force can also expand production capabilities. This outward shift represents economic growth – the ability to produce more of both goods.

Conversely, factors that decrease resource availability or hinder production efficiency can shift the PPF inwards, shrinking the range of attainable outputs. Natural disasters, depletion of resources, or economic downturns can all lead to a contraction of the production possibilities. This inward shift represents a decline in the economy's productive capacity.

The PPF is not just a theoretical concept; it has practical implications for businesses and individuals. Businesses use similar principles to analyze their production choices. A furniture manufacturer, for example, might use a PPF-like model to decide how many chairs versus tables to produce given their limited wood, labor, and machinery. Understanding opportunity cost helps them maximize their output and profitability.

Individuals also face production possibilities frontiers in their daily lives. We all have limited time and energy. Choosing to spend time on one activity, like studying, means less time available for other activities, like socializing or exercising. Recognizing these trade-offs allows us to make more conscious choices about how we allocate our limited resources, whether those resources are time, money, or effort.

Efficient resource allocation is not just about maximizing output; it's also about achieving desired outcomes. The PPF provides a framework for understanding the trade-offs involved in production decisions and making choices that align with our goals. By carefully considering opportunity costs and striving for efficiency, we can move closer to the frontier of our production possibilities and make the most of our limited resources. This careful allocation, coupled with a drive for innovation and growth, is key to achieving economic prosperity and improving our overall well-being. It's about understanding the constraints and working within them to achieve the best possible outcomes. It's about making informed choices that move us closer to our desired future.

1.4 Economic Systems

Understanding how societies organize their resources is fundamental to grasping the complexities of global trade, development, and individual prosperity. Different economic systems prioritize different values and lead to distinct outcomes in terms of wealth distribution, innovation, and social welfare. These aren't merely theoretical models, but living, breathing structures that shape our daily lives.

One of the oldest and simplest forms of economic organization is the traditional economy. Often found in rural or indigenous communities, it relies on customs, traditions, and inherited roles to determine what is produced, how it's produced, and for whom. Think of a family farm passed down through generations, where everyone has a predetermined role, and production primarily serves the immediate community. Bartering, rather than currency-based exchange, is often prevalent. While these systems offer stability and a strong sense of community, they often resist change and can limit economic growth and individual advancement. Innovation is often stifled, as methods are passed down unchanged through time, leading to a lower overall standard of living compared to other systems.

In contrast, market economies prioritize individual choice and free enterprise. Decisions regarding production and consumption are decentralized, driven by the forces of supply and demand. Prices act as signals, guiding resources towards their most valued uses. Competition among producers encourages innovation and efficiency, leading to a wider variety of goods and services and often, lower prices. Individuals are incentivized to work hard and innovate, as they directly benefit from their efforts. This system fosters dynamic growth, technological advancements, and adaptability to changing circumstances. However, pure market economies can lead to significant income inequality and may fail to provide essential goods and services to those who cannot afford them. Unregulated markets can also be susceptible to boom and bust cycles and environmental degradation.

Moving along the spectrum of economic organization, we find command economies, also known as centrally planned economies. In this system, the government controls the means of production and makes decisions about what to produce, how to produce it, and how to distribute goods and services.

This centralized approach can, theoretically, lead to rapid mobilization of resources for specific national goals, such as industrialization or infrastructure development. It can also ensure a more equitable distribution of basic necessities. However, command economies often struggle with inefficiency, lack of innovation, and shortages of consumer goods. The absence of market signals and competition can lead to misallocation of resources and a lack of responsiveness to consumer preferences. Furthermore, centralized control can stifle individual initiative and create an environment ripe for corruption.

Most real-world economies are mixed economies, combining elements of market and command systems. Governments in these systems typically intervene to regulate markets, provide public goods and services, redistribute income, and stabilize the economy. The degree of government intervention varies significantly across countries, creating a diverse landscape of mixed economies. For example, some countries, like the Scandinavian nations, prioritize social welfare and have robust safety nets, while others, like the United States, emphasize market forces and have a relatively smaller public sector. The balance between market and government influence is constantly evolving and subject to political and societal debates.

The rise of globalization has further complicated the landscape of economic systems. Increased international trade, investment, and migration have interconnected national economies, creating a complex web of interdependence. This has led to both opportunities and challenges. On the one hand, globalization has fostered economic growth, increased access to goods and services, and facilitated the spread of technology and ideas. On the other hand, it has also raised concerns about job displacement, environmental degradation, and the erosion of national sovereignty. Managing the complexities of globalization requires international cooperation and a nuanced understanding of the interplay between different economic systems.

Understanding the strengths and weaknesses of various economic systems is crucial for navigating the global landscape. Each system offers a unique set of advantages and disadvantages, and the choice of which system to adopt or how to mix elements of different systems is a complex one with significant societal implications. There is no one-size-fits-all solution, and the optimal approach depends on a variety of factors, including a nation's history, culture, resources, and political values.

Consider the implications of resource allocation. In a market economy, resources are allocated based on price signals, reflecting consumer preferences and producer costs. In a command economy, the government decides how resources are allocated, potentially prioritizing national interests over individual needs. In a traditional economy, resource allocation is often determined by custom and inheritance. Each approach has its own set of trade-offs in terms of efficiency, equity, and sustainability.

Furthermore, the level of economic freedom and individual initiative varies significantly across different systems. Market economies generally offer greater economic freedom, allowing individuals to pursue their own self-interest and innovate without government interference. Command economies, on the other hand, restrict individual freedom in favor of centralized planning. Traditional economies often limit individual choices based on established social roles and customs. The balance between individual freedom and collective goals is a central tension in the design of any economic system.

Finally, it's important to remember that economic systems are not static. They evolve over time, influenced by technological advancements, changing social values, and global events. Understanding the dynamics of economic systems is essential for anticipating future trends and adapting to the challenges and opportunities of a constantly changing world. By studying the various systems, their strengths and weaknesses, and the ways they interact, we gain valuable insights into the forces that shape our economic lives.

1.5 The Role of Incentives

Understanding human motivation is key to effective leadership and organizational success. We are all driven by a complex interplay of desires, needs, and aspirations. Incentives tap into this intricate web, offering a powerful tool to shape behavior and drive performance. They provide the "why" behind the "what," influencing our choices and actions in profound ways. Effectively designed incentive systems can be the cornerstone of a thriving and productive environment.

Think about a time you were truly motivated to achieve a goal. What drove you? Perhaps it was the promise of a reward, the satisfaction of mastering a new skill, or the desire to contribute to something larger than yourself. These are all examples of incentives at play. They can be tangible, like bonuses or promotions, or intangible, such as recognition and praise. The key is to understand what resonates with individuals and aligns with organizational objectives.

The most effective incentives are not one-size-fits-all. They are tailored to the specific needs and preferences of the individuals they aim to motivate. A recent study highlighted the effectiveness of personalized incentive programs in boosting employee engagement. The research showed that employees who felt their incentives were tailored to their individual contributions were significantly more likely to exceed performance expectations. This personalization requires careful consideration of individual motivations, career aspirations, and even personal circumstances.

Consider a sales team, for example. While some team members may be highly motivated by financial rewards, others might prioritize opportunities for professional development or greater autonomy in their work. A successful incentive program would offer a mix of options, allowing individuals to choose the rewards that best align with their personal goals. This approach not only maximizes motivation but also fosters a sense of ownership and commitment.

Furthermore, the timing and frequency of incentives play a crucial role in their effectiveness. Immediate rewards tend to have a stronger impact than those offered far in the future. This is due to the psychological principle of temporal discounting, which suggests that we value immediate rewards more highly than delayed ones. Frequent, smaller incentives can also be more effective than infrequent, larger ones, as they maintain a consistent level of motivation and provide regular reinforcement of desired behaviors.

Transparency and fairness are also paramount in designing effective incentive systems. Employees need to understand how the system works, what criteria are used to determine rewards, and how their performance is being evaluated. A lack of transparency can breed distrust and resentment, undermining the very purpose of the incentive program. Regular communication and open feedback mechanisms are essential to ensure that everyone feels valued and understands the connection between their efforts and their rewards.

Incentives can also be used to foster collaboration and teamwork. Team-based incentives encourage individuals to work together towards a common goal, promoting a sense of shared responsibility and collective achievement. However, it's crucial to design these incentives carefully to avoid creating unhealthy competition or incentivizing individuals to prioritize their own gains over the team's success. A well-structured team-based incentive program should reward collective performance while also recognizing individual contributions.

Beyond monetary rewards and promotions, non-financial incentives can be incredibly powerful. Recognition, praise, and opportunities for professional development can significantly impact employee motivation and engagement. A simple "thank you" or a public acknowledgment of a job well done can go a long way in boosting morale and reinforcing positive behaviors. Offering opportunities for skill development, mentorship programs, or challenging assignments can also be highly motivating, demonstrating a commitment to employee growth and career advancement.

The effectiveness of any incentive program hinges on its alignment with organizational values and overall strategy. Incentives should reinforce desired behaviors and contribute to the achievement of overarching business goals. If incentives are misaligned, they can inadvertently encourage counterproductive behaviors or undermine the organization's mission. For instance, if a company prioritizes customer satisfaction but primarily incentivizes sales volume, employees may be tempted to prioritize closing deals over building long-term customer relationships.

Finally, it's essential to regularly evaluate and adjust incentive programs. The needs and motivations of individuals can change over time, and what once worked effectively may no longer be as impactful. Regularly gathering feedback from employees, tracking program performance, and making necessary adjustments are crucial to ensuring that incentives remain relevant and effective in driving desired outcomes. A dynamic approach to incentive design allows organizations to adapt to evolving circumstances and maximize the motivational power of their reward systems. By understanding the nuances of human motivation and tailoring incentives accordingly, organizations can create a culture of high performance, engagement, and shared success. This ongoing process of refinement and adaptation is key to unlocking the full potential of incentives and driving sustainable organizational growth.

2 Microeconomic Principles

At its core, microeconomics examines how individual economic agents—households, firms, and even individuals—make decisions in the face of scarcity. These decisions, seemingly small and isolated, aggregate to form the complex tapestry of market interactions that determine prices, output, and resource allocation. Understanding these individual motivations and the mechanisms through which they interact is crucial for grasping the broader economic landscape. Consider, for example, a farmer deciding how much wheat to plant, a family choosing between a vacation and a new car, or a business owner determining the optimal number of employees to hire. Each of these choices, governed by the principles of microeconomics, contributes to the overall economic activity within a market.

The cornerstone of microeconomic analysis lies in the concepts of supply and demand. Supply represents the willingness and ability of producers to offer goods and services at different price points. Several factors influence supply, including production costs, technology, and government regulations. A technological advancement that lowers the cost of producing computer chips, for instance, will likely increase the supply of chips at any given price. Demand, on the other hand, reflects the desire and ability of consumers to purchase goods and services at various prices. Consumer preferences, income levels, and the prices of related goods all play a role in shaping demand. For example, a rise in consumer incomes might increase the demand for luxury goods. The intersection of these two forces, supply and demand, determines the market equilibrium—the price at which the quantity supplied equals the quantity demanded. This equilibrium point represents a balance of forces, where buyers and sellers agree on a price and quantity that clears the market.

Moving beyond the basic supply and demand framework, the concept of elasticity provides a more nuanced understanding of market responsiveness. Elasticity measures the percentage change in one variable (like quantity demanded or supplied) in response to a percentage change in another variable (like price or income). Price elasticity of demand, for instance, quantifies how sensitive the quantity demanded of a good is to changes in its price. A good with high price elasticity of demand will experience a significant decrease in quantity demanded when its price increases, suggesting consumers have readily available substitutes. Conversely, a good with low price elasticity of demand, like gasoline or essential medications, will see a smaller change in quantity demanded even with significant price fluctuations, as consumers have fewer alternatives. Understanding elasticity is crucial for businesses in setting prices, forecasting sales, and responding to changes in market conditions. Governments also use elasticity measures to predict the impact of taxes or subsidies.

Market structures, another key element of microeconomics, describe the competitive landscape within which firms operate. These structures range from perfect competition, characterized by numerous small firms selling identical products, to monopoly, where a single firm dominates the entire market. Between these two extremes lie oligopoly, involving a few large firms with significant market power, and monopolistic competition, where many firms offer differentiated products. Each market structure presents unique challenges and opportunities for businesses. In a perfectly competitive market, firms have little control over price and must focus on cost efficiency to survive. In contrast, a monopolist has significant pricing power but may face regulatory scrutiny. The structure of a market significantly impacts pricing strategies, output levels, and ultimately, profitability. Analyzing market structures allows economists to understand the dynamics of competition and its impact on consumer welfare.

Delving into consumer behavior, microeconomics explores how individuals make decisions based on their preferences, budget constraints, and the available information. Consumers aim to maximize their utility, or satisfaction, given their limited resources. This involves making trade-offs and choosing the combination of goods and services that best satisfies their needs and wants. Consider a student deciding how to allocate their limited study time across different subjects. They will likely prioritize subjects that are more difficult or carry more weight in their overall grade, aiming to maximize their academic performance given their time constraints. Understanding consumer behavior helps businesses tailor their products and marketing strategies to effectively reach their target audiences.

Production theory, another essential aspect of microeconomics, examines how firms combine inputs, such as labor, capital, and raw materials, to produce output. Firms aim to minimize their production costs while maximizing output, leading to concepts like economies of scale and efficient production techniques. A manufacturing company, for example, might invest in automation to reduce labor costs and increase production efficiency. Analyzing production theory helps businesses make informed decisions about resource allocation, technology adoption, and optimal output levels. This understanding contributes to improved efficiency and profitability within individual firms and the broader economy.

Finally, microeconomics also considers the role of externalities, which are costs or benefits imposed on third parties not directly involved in a transaction. Pollution from a factory affecting nearby residents is a classic example of a negative externality. Conversely, a beekeeper's bees pollinating neighboring crops represents a positive externality. Understanding externalities is crucial for designing policies that address market failures and promote social welfare. Governments might implement taxes or regulations to discourage activities with negative externalities, while subsidies can encourage activities with positive externalities, leading to a more efficient and equitable allocation of resources. By examining these various aspects, microeconomics provides a framework for understanding the intricate workings of individual markets and their impact on the broader economy.

2.1 Supply and Demand

The dance between supply and demand dictates the rhythm of the market. It's a fundamental principle, a constant push and pull that influences everything from the price of bread to the availability of skilled labor. Understanding this interplay is crucial for navigating the complexities of any economic system. We'll delve into the intricacies of this relationship, exploring how these forces interact to shape market outcomes. This understanding can empower you to make informed decisions, whether you're running a business, investing your money, or simply trying to understand the world around you. Supply represents the quantity of a good or service that producers are willing and able to offer at various price points. Think of a local farmer's market. A farmer bringing their harvest to sell represents the supply of, say, tomatoes. The higher the price they can fetch for their tomatoes, the more they're incentivized to bring to market. This illustrates the basic principle of the supply curve: as price increases, so does the quantity supplied. Conversely, if tomato prices plummet, the farmer might choose to sell fewer, perhaps using the remainder for canning or letting them rot on the vine. This isn't simply about profit; it's about efficient resource allocation.

Demand, on the other hand, reflects the consumer's desire and ability to purchase a good or service at a particular price. Imagine shoppers at that same farmer's market looking for ripe tomatoes. Some might be willing to pay a premium for the best-looking produce, while others are more price-sensitive. Generally, the lower the price, the higher the demand. This is the law of demand in action. A sudden drop in tomato prices might lead to a surge in purchases – everyone loves a bargain. However, if prices skyrocket, consumers might opt for alternatives, like canned tomatoes or other vegetables.

The point where supply and demand intersect is the market equilibrium. This is the sweet spot where the quantity supplied equals the quantity demanded. At this price, there's no surplus (excess supply) or shortage (excess demand). Everyone who wants to buy at that price can find a seller, and every seller can find a buyer. This equilibrium price isn't static; it's constantly adjusting to changes in market conditions.

Numerous factors can influence both supply and demand, shifting their respective curves and ultimately affecting the equilibrium price. Consider weather patterns. A late frost could devastate the tomato crop, drastically reducing supply and pushing prices higher. Conversely, a bumper crop could lead to a glut of tomatoes, forcing prices down. On the demand side, factors like consumer preferences, income levels, and the prices of related goods (like substitutes or complements) can all play a role. A sudden craze for tomato-based recipes could increase demand, while a recession could decrease it.

Understanding these dynamics is crucial for businesses. A company that misjudges demand could end up with overflowing warehouses or empty shelves. Accurate forecasting and a keen awareness of market trends are essential for success. For investors, understanding supply and demand can help predict price movements and identify promising opportunities. For example, anticipating a shortage of a particular commodity could lead to a profitable investment.

Let's look at a hypothetical example. Imagine a new smartphone hits the market. Initially, supply is limited, but demand is high due to the innovative features. This creates a situation where the price is relatively high. As production ramps up, supply increases. If demand remains constant, this increase in supply will push the price down. However, if the phone proves immensely popular, demand could increase even faster than supply, leading to even higher prices.

This dynamic interplay between supply and demand isn't

confined to tangible goods. It also applies to services, labor markets, and even financial assets. The principles remain the same: scarcity and desirability drive prices. The availability of skilled workers in a particular field, for example, influences wages. A shortage of software developers, coupled with high demand, leads to higher salaries.

Mastering the concepts of supply and demand is like learning the language of the market. It provides a framework for understanding how prices are determined, how resources are allocated, and how economic forces shape our world. By recognizing the interplay of these fundamental principles, we can make more informed decisions as consumers, producers, and investors. This knowledge empowers us to navigate the complexities of the market with greater confidence and understanding, enabling us to anticipate trends and capitalize on opportunities.

The ability to analyze market conditions through the lens of supply and demand offers a significant advantage. It allows us to anticipate potential price fluctuations and understand the underlying reasons behind them. This understanding can inform our decisions, whether we're deciding when to buy a new car, invest in a particular stock, or start a new business. It's a powerful tool for anyone seeking to navigate the intricacies of the economic landscape. Remember, the market is constantly evolving, and the forces of supply and demand are always at play. By understanding these forces, we can better position ourselves for success.

2.2 Elasticity and Its Applications

We encounter elasticity everywhere, often without realizing it. From the slight give of a wooden floor to the bounce of a rubber ball, this fundamental property of materials governs how objects deform and return to their original shape when subjected to forces. Understanding elasticity is key to designing safe and functional structures, from bridges spanning vast distances to the tiny springs inside your pen. It's a concept that intertwines physics and engineering, impacting nearly every aspect of the designed world around us.

Elasticity is formally defined as the ability of a material to resist deformation and return to its original shape after a force is removed. This "resistance" isn't simply about strength; a strong material might deform permanently under stress. Instead, elasticity is about the material's tendency to "spring back." This behavior is driven by the atomic and molecular structure of the material. When a force is applied, these internal bonds stretch or compress. If the force isn't too great, the bonds return to their original configuration once the force is removed, and the material regains its original shape.

Consider a simple rubber band. Pulling on it stretches the long, tangled polymer chains within the rubber. These chains are like tiny springs, wanting to recoil back to their resting state. When you release the rubber band, these internal forces pull the material back to its original length. This is a classic example of elastic behavior. However, if you stretch the rubber band too far, you can permanently deform it, exceeding its elastic limit. This demonstrates a crucial point: elasticity has its limits. Beyond a certain point, called the yield strength, the material will deform permanently, or even fracture.

The mathematical framework for describing elasticity revolves around stress and strain. Stress is the force applied per unit area, while strain is the deformation resulting from that stress. For many materials, within their elastic limit, the relationship between stress and strain is linear. This relationship is known as Hooke's Law, and it's foundational to understanding and predicting elastic behavior. The proportionality constant in Hooke's Law is called the modulus of elasticity, often referred to as Young's modulus. This modulus represents the stiffness of a material, a measure of how much stress is required to produce a given amount of strain.

A higher modulus of elasticity means a stiffer material, one that resists deformation more strongly. Steel, for instance, has a much higher modulus of elasticity than rubber, reflecting its greater stiffness. This difference in stiffness is why steel is used for building skyscrapers, while rubber is used for car tires. The application dictates the material's required elastic properties.

The concept of elasticity extends beyond simple stretching and compression. It also encompasses shear stress, which occurs when forces are applied parallel to a surface, causing one layer of the material to slide over another. Think of spreading a deck of cards – the cards slide against each other, experiencing shear stress. The resistance to this type of deformation is characterized by the shear modulus, another important material property.

Understanding these different moduli allows engineers to predict how materials will behave under various loading conditions. This is critical for designing everything from aircraft wings that must withstand aerodynamic forces to the suspension systems in cars that absorb bumps in the road. The choice of materials and their specific elastic properties is a crucial consideration in ensuring the safety and functionality of any engineered structure.

Furthermore, elasticity plays a vital role in many other areas. In seismology, the elastic properties of rocks are studied to understand how seismic waves propagate through the Earth. In medical imaging, ultrasound relies on the elastic properties of tissues to create images of internal organs. Even the musical tones produced by a guitar string are a result of the string's elasticity and its ability to vibrate at specific frequencies.

The study of elasticity is a rich and complex field with wide-ranging applications. From the macroscopic world of bridges and buildings to the microscopic realm of materials science and nanotechnology, the principles of elasticity are fundamental to understanding how the world around us behaves. By grasping the concepts of stress, strain, and the various moduli, we gain a powerful tool for designing, analyzing, and appreciating the intricate interplay of forces and materials that shapes our world. This knowledge allows us to not only build stronger and more resilient structures but also to appreciate the subtle ways in which elasticity manifests itself in everyday phenomena.

Considering the dynamic nature of forces and the varied responses of materials, understanding the limits of elasticity is paramount. Beyond the elastic limit, materials enter the plastic region, where deformation becomes permanent. This transition marks a critical point in the behavior of a material under stress. Knowing the yield strength and the ultimate tensile strength, the maximum stress a material can withstand before fracturing, is essential for ensuring structural integrity. These properties, alongside the elastic moduli, provide a comprehensive picture of a material's mechanical behavior. They form the basis for selecting appropriate materials for specific applications and designing structures that can safely withstand the forces they are subjected to. The intricate interplay of elasticity and its limits defines the boundaries of material performance, impacting everything from the durability of a bridge to the resilience of a surgical implant.

2.3 Market Structures

Understanding market structures is fundamental to navigating the business landscape. Each structure presents unique opportunities and challenges, influencing pricing strategies, competitive dynamics, and ultimately, profitability. By recognizing the characteristics of different market structures, businesses can tailor their approaches to maximize their chances of success. This analysis provides a framework for dissecting these structures and their implications.

A perfectly competitive market is often considered the ideal, though rarely achieved in reality. Numerous small firms offer identical products, and no single entity holds sway over the market price. Think of agricultural commodities like wheat or corn – thousands of farmers contribute to the overall supply, with each individual farmer having a negligible impact on the market price. Entry and exit are frictionless, allowing new businesses to emerge easily and struggling businesses to depart without significant barriers. Perfect information is assumed, meaning all participants have equal access to market data. While true perfect competition is rare, understanding its characteristics provides a valuable benchmark for analyzing real-world markets. This theoretical model helps illuminate the forces of supply and demand in their purest form.

In contrast, a monopoly exists when a single firm dominates an entire market. This firm becomes the sole provider of a product or service with no close substitutes. This dominance allows the monopolist to control prices and output, potentially leading to higher prices and lower quantities compared to a competitive market. Barriers to entry are significant, preventing other firms from entering and competing. These barriers can include patents, exclusive access to resources, or government regulations. Utility companies often exemplify this structure, with a single provider serving a specific geographic area. Analyzing monopolies involves understanding the potential for market inefficiency and the role of regulation in mitigating its negative consequences.

Oligopolies represent a middle ground between perfect competition and monopolies. A few large firms dominate the market, each holding a substantial market share. Think of the automobile industry or the airline industry, where a handful of major players compete. The actions of one firm directly influence the others, creating interdependence. This can lead to complex strategic interactions, including price wars, collusion, and product differentiation. Barriers to entry, while not as absolute as in monopolies, are still significant. Analyzing oligopolies requires understanding game theory, strategic behavior, and the potential for both competition and cooperation.

Monopolistic competition, often confused with perfect competition, involves many firms selling differentiated products. While numerous businesses operate within the market, each firm offers a slightly different product or service. This differentiation allows firms to exert some control over their prices. Restaurants, clothing stores, and salons often fall under this category. Each business might offer similar services, but variations in style, quality, or location create distinct market niches. Entry and exit are relatively easy, allowing for a dynamic and evolving market landscape. Analyzing monopolistic competition focuses on the role of product differentiation, branding, and customer loyalty in shaping market outcomes.

Understanding the interplay of these market structures provides crucial insights for businesses. Recognizing the specific structure in which you operate allows you to tailor your strategies accordingly. For instance, in a highly competitive market, focusing on cost efficiency and providing value to consumers is paramount. In an oligopoly, understanding your competitors' strategies and anticipating their reactions is critical. In a monopolistic competition, establishing a strong brand and differentiating your offering are key to success.

Beyond simply identifying the current market structure, it's vital to consider the potential for change. Markets are dynamic, and structures can evolve over time. Technological advancements, regulatory changes, and shifts in consumer preferences can all disrupt existing market structures. For instance, the rise of the internet has transformed numerous industries, breaking down geographical barriers and increasing competition. Businesses need to be adaptable and anticipate these changes to maintain their competitive edge.

Furthermore, the interplay between different market structures can be complex. A firm might operate in a highly competitive market for some of its products while enjoying a near-monopoly in another. For example, a large technology company might face fierce competition in its smartphone division but hold a dominant position in its operating system market. Recognizing these nuances is essential for developing effective strategies across different product lines.

Market structure analysis isn't a one-time exercise; it's an ongoing process. As markets evolve, businesses need to continuously reassess their competitive landscape. This involves monitoring industry trends, analyzing competitor behavior, and understanding the changing needs of consumers. By staying informed and adaptable, businesses can navigate the complexities of the market and position themselves for long-term success. Through a thorough understanding of market structures, businesses can make informed decisions about pricing, product development, marketing, and overall competitive strategy, ultimately enhancing their profitability and sustainability in a dynamic global marketplace. Recognizing the specific forces at play within each structure empowers businesses to adapt and thrive. This knowledge translates into a powerful tool for navigating the complexities of the business world.

3 Macroeconomic Forces

The world economy is a complex interplay of various forces. Understanding these forces is crucial for navigating the financial landscape. This chapter delves into the core concepts of macroeconomics, providing a framework for comprehending the dynamics that shape national and global economies. We'll explore how these concepts intertwine and influence our financial well-being. Think of the economy as a giant engine with multiple interconnected parts, each playing a critical role in the overall functioning of the system.

Gross Domestic Product (GDP) serves as a primary indicator of a nation's economic health. It represents the total value of all goods and services produced within a country's borders during a specific period. GDP growth signifies an expanding economy, typically associated with increased employment opportunities and rising incomes. However, relying solely on GDP can be misleading, as it doesn't account for income inequality or environmental sustainability. A more nuanced approach considers factors like the Gini coefficient, which measures income distribution, and the Human Development Index (HDI), reflecting overall well-being. Imagine a car with a powerful engine but faulty brakes – while the engine might be impressive, the lack of safety features diminishes its overall value. Similarly, a country with high GDP but significant inequality or environmental damage faces hidden vulnerabilities.

Unemployment, representing the percentage of the labor force actively seeking employment but unable to find it, is another key macroeconomic indicator. High unemployment rates can lead to social unrest and economic stagnation. Different types of unemployment exist, including frictional (temporary unemployment during job transitions), structural (mismatch between skills and available jobs), and cyclical (fluctuations related to the business cycle). Understanding these distinctions helps policymakers design targeted interventions. Consider a factory replacing workers with automated machines – this contributes to structural unemployment, requiring retraining programs to equip workers with new skills for different industries.

Inflation, the sustained increase in the general price level of goods and services in an economy over a period, erodes purchasing power and can destabilize economic growth. Various factors contribute to inflation, including increased demand, rising production costs, and expansionary monetary policy. Governments and central banks strive to maintain a stable inflation rate, typically around 2%, to foster predictable economic conditions. Think of inflation like air slowly leaking out of a tire – over time, it weakens the tire's performance, just as inflation gradually diminishes the value of money.

Governments employ fiscal policy, which involves adjusting government spending and taxation, to influence the economy. Expansionary fiscal policy, increasing government spending or cutting taxes, stimulates economic activity during recessions. Conversely, contractionary fiscal policy, decreasing spending or raising taxes, helps control inflation during periods of rapid economic growth. Imagine a gardener watering plants during a dry spell (expansionary policy) and pruning them when they grow too rapidly (contractionary policy). Fiscal policy acts as a similar regulating force within the economy.

Central banks, independent institutions responsible for managing a nation's monetary policy, primarily control the money supply and interest rates. Lowering interest rates encourages borrowing and investment, stimulating economic activity. Raising interest rates curbs inflation by reducing borrowing and spending. The interplay between fiscal and monetary policy is crucial for maintaining economic stability. Think of monetary policy as adjusting the thermostat of the economy – central banks aim to maintain a comfortable temperature by controlling the flow of money, much like a thermostat regulates the flow of heat or cool air.

International trade, the exchange of goods and services across national borders, offers numerous benefits, including increased efficiency, access to a wider variety of goods, and lower prices for consumers. However, it also presents challenges, such as trade imbalances and potential job displacement in certain industries. Understanding the complexities of international trade requires considering factors like comparative advantage, trade barriers (tariffs and quotas), and exchange rates. Imagine a world where each country specializes in producing what it does best – this is the essence of comparative advantage, leading to increased global output and greater overall prosperity.

Economic development, a broader concept than economic growth, encompasses improvements in living standards, education, healthcare, and infrastructure. It focuses on enhancing the overall quality of life for individuals within a society. Factors contributing to economic development include investments in human capital, technological advancements, and sound institutional frameworks. Think of economic development as building a sturdy house – it requires a strong foundation (education and healthcare), reliable utilities (infrastructure), and ongoing maintenance (good governance) to ensure long-term well-being.

Comprehending these macroeconomic forces provides a foundational understanding of how national and global economies function. This knowledge empowers individuals to make informed financial decisions and navigate the complexities of the ever-evolving financial landscape. By recognizing the interconnectedness of these forces, we gain valuable insights into the mechanisms driving economic growth, stability, and ultimately, our own financial well-being. Just as a skilled mechanic understands the workings of an engine, a financially literate individual comprehends the forces shaping the economic machinery, enabling them to navigate the road to financial success.

3.1 GDP and Economic Growth

Understanding a nation's economic health is like taking its pulse. One of the most common ways we measure this health is by looking at its Gross Domestic Product, or GDP. This metric essentially sums up the total value of all the goods and services a country produces within a specific timeframe, typically a year. It's a snapshot, offering a glimpse into the size and performance of an economy. Think of it as a country's economic report card.

GDP provides valuable insights, allowing us to compare economic performance across different countries and track changes over time within a single nation. It helps policymakers make informed decisions about taxes, spending, and interest rates. Businesses use GDP data to forecast demand and plan investments. Investors rely on it to assess market conditions and make strategic decisions about where to allocate their capital. A growing GDP generally signals a healthy economy, one where businesses are thriving, people are employed, and incomes are rising.

There are three main ways to calculate GDP: the expenditure approach, the income approach, and the production (or value-added) approach. The expenditure approach sums up all spending on final goods and services within an economy. This includes consumer spending, business investment, government spending, and net exports (exports minus imports). The income approach tallies up all the income earned in the production of goods and services, including wages, salaries, profits, and rents. Finally, the production approach calculates the value added at each stage of production, from raw materials to the final product. Remarkably, while each approach takes a different perspective, they all arrive at the same GDP figure.

However, GDP is not without its limitations. It doesn't capture the value of unpaid work, such as household chores or volunteer activities. It also fails to account for the depletion of natural resources or the negative impacts of pollution. Furthermore, GDP doesn't reflect the distribution of income within a country. A country with a high GDP might still have significant income inequality, with a small percentage of the population holding a large share of the wealth. These shortcomings highlight the importance of considering other factors, such as social well-being and environmental sustainability, alongside GDP when assessing a nation's overall progress.

Economic growth, often measured as the percentage change in GDP over time, represents a sustained increase in a nation's production of goods and services. This growth is essential for improving living standards, creating jobs, and generating the resources needed to address societal challenges like poverty and healthcare. Several factors contribute to economic growth. Technological advancements can lead to increased productivity and efficiency, allowing businesses to produce more with fewer resources. Investments in physical capital, such as machinery and infrastructure, create a foundation for future growth. Human capital, including education and skills development, empowers individuals to contribute more effectively to the economy. A stable political and economic environment fosters confidence and encourages investment, while open trade policies can expand markets and promote competition.

Understanding the relationship between GDP and economic growth is crucial. A growing GDP indicates that an economy is expanding, producing more goods and services, and creating jobs. This expansion can lead to higher incomes, increased consumer spending, and further investment, creating a virtuous cycle of growth. However, it's important to note that economic growth can be unevenly distributed across different sectors of the economy and different segments of the population. Therefore, policymakers need to implement strategies that promote inclusive growth, ensuring that the benefits are shared by all members of society.

Analyzing long-term economic growth patterns reveals interesting trends. Some countries have experienced rapid growth over extended periods, transforming from developing economies to global economic powerhouses. Others have struggled with slow growth or even periods of decline. Factors influencing these long-term trends include a country's institutions, its access to resources, its level of technological innovation, and its demographic characteristics. For example, countries with strong institutions, well-defined property rights, and efficient legal systems tend to attract more investment and experience faster growth.

Sustained economic growth requires a delicate balance between various economic factors. Excessive inflation can erode purchasing power and stifle investment. High unemployment can lead to social unrest and decreased consumer spending. Large trade deficits can weaken a nation's currency and increase its dependence on foreign capital. Policymakers use a variety of tools, including monetary policy and fiscal policy, to manage these challenges and maintain a stable economic environment conducive to growth. Monetary policy involves manipulating interest rates and the money supply to

control inflation and influence economic activity. Fiscal policy involves adjusting government spending and taxation to stimulate or cool down the economy.
While GDP and economic growth are essential indicators of a nation's economic performance, they are not the sole determinants of its overall well-being. Other factors, such as income distribution, access to healthcare and education, environmental sustainability, and social justice, play a vital role in determining the quality of life for its citizens. A truly prosperous nation is one that not only achieves economic growth but also ensures that the benefits of that growth are shared widely and sustainably. Striking the right balance between economic growth and other societal goals is the key to building a thriving and equitable future for all. Understanding the intricacies of GDP and economic growth is essential for anyone seeking to navigate the complexities of the modern global economy.

3.2 Unemployment and Inflation

The intertwined dance of unemployment and inflation is a complex waltz that economists have been studying for centuries. One of the most widely accepted relationships between these two economic forces is the Phillips Curve, which suggests an inverse relationship: low unemployment often coincides with higher inflation, and vice versa. Imagine a bustling economy where businesses are scrambling to hire workers. In this competitive labor market, wages rise, pushing up production costs and ultimately the prices consumers pay for goods and services. Conversely, during periods of high unemployment, demand for goods and services tends to be weaker, leading to slower price growth or even deflation. However, this relationship is not always straightforward, and the real world often presents more nuanced scenarios.

One such scenario is stagflation, a dreaded combination of stagnant economic growth, high unemployment, and persistent inflation. The 1970s oil crisis provides a prime example. The sharp rise in oil prices triggered a surge in inflation, while simultaneously slowing down economic activity and leading to job losses. This scenario challenged the traditional Phillips Curve relationship, demonstrating that external shocks can disrupt the delicate balance between unemployment and inflation. Understanding these complexities is crucial for policymakers who aim to steer the economy toward stable growth and full employment.

Navigating these economic crosscurrents requires careful consideration of various factors influencing both unemployment and inflation. Demand-pull inflation arises when overall demand in the economy outpaces the capacity to produce goods and services. This can occur during periods of strong economic growth or expansionary fiscal policy. Think of it as too much money chasing too few goods. On the other hand, cost-push inflation stems from increases in production costs, such as rising wages or raw material prices. These increased costs are then passed on to consumers in the form of higher prices. Understanding the specific drivers of inflation is crucial for crafting appropriate policy responses.

Unemployment, too, has various forms and underlying causes. Frictional unemployment, for instance, is a natural consequence of people transitioning between jobs. It represents the time it takes for workers to find new employment that matches their skills and preferences. Structural unemployment, however, is a more persistent issue, arising from mismatches between the skills of the workforce and the demands of the labor market. Technological advancements, for example, can render certain skills obsolete, leaving workers unemployed unless they acquire new skills. Cyclical unemployment, tied to the ebb and flow of the business cycle, occurs during economic downturns when businesses reduce production and lay off workers.

Policymakers employ a range of tools to address unemployment and inflation. Monetary policy, controlled by central banks, primarily influences interest rates. By raising interest rates, central banks can cool down an overheating economy and curb inflation by making borrowing more expensive and reducing consumer spending. Conversely, lowering interest rates can stimulate economic activity and reduce unemployment by encouraging investment and consumer spending. Fiscal policy, the domain of governments, involves adjustments to government spending and taxation. Tax cuts can boost disposable income and stimulate demand, while increased government spending on infrastructure projects, for example, can create jobs and spur economic growth.

The effectiveness of these policies depends on a multitude of factors, including the specific economic context, the timing of interventions, and the interplay between various economic forces. For instance, expansionary fiscal policy during a period of high inflation could exacerbate inflationary pressures. Similarly, lowering interest rates when inflation is already rampant could further fuel price increases. Finding the right balance and tailoring policies to the specific circumstances is a constant challenge for policymakers.

Beyond these macroeconomic tools, supply-side policies aim

to enhance the productive capacity of the economy. These policies can include investments in education and training to improve the skills of the workforce, deregulation to reduce barriers to business entry and competition, and infrastructure development to improve transportation and communication networks. By increasing productivity and efficiency, supply-side policies can contribute to long-term sustainable economic growth and mitigate inflationary pressures.

Another critical aspect of managing unemployment and inflation is managing expectations. If businesses and consumers anticipate rising inflation, they may adjust their behavior accordingly. Businesses might raise prices in anticipation of higher costs, while consumers might rush to purchase goods before prices rise further, creating a self-fulfilling prophecy of inflation. Similarly, persistent high unemployment can lead to a decline in worker morale and a reduction in investment, exacerbating economic stagnation. Therefore, maintaining public confidence in the stability of the economy is crucial for effective policy implementation.

Finally, recognizing the global interconnectedness of economies is essential. International trade, capital flows, and exchange rates all influence domestic economic conditions. External shocks, such as global recessions or commodity price fluctuations, can significantly impact both unemployment and inflation. Therefore, policymakers must consider these global factors when formulating economic policies.

In conclusion, understanding the dynamic relationship between unemployment and inflation is fundamental for navigating the complexities of the modern economy. Recognizing the various factors influencing these two crucial economic indicators, employing appropriate policy tools, and managing expectations are all essential for achieving sustainable economic growth and full employment. The ongoing challenge for policymakers is to find the right balance between stimulating economic activity and maintaining price stability, a task that requires constant vigilance and adaptation to ever-changing economic conditions.

3.3 Fiscal and Monetary Policy

Understanding the interplay between fiscal and monetary policy is crucial for navigating the complexities of a nation's economy. These two powerful tools, wielded by different authorities, influence everything from inflation and unemployment to economic growth and stability. They are distinct yet interconnected, working in concert to steer the economic ship.

A well-coordinated approach can lead to prosperity, while misaligned policies can cause significant turbulence.

Fiscal policy, the domain of the government, focuses on influencing the economy through adjustments in government spending and taxation. Consider a government facing a recession. They might increase spending on infrastructure projects, creating jobs and injecting money into the economy. Alternatively, they could cut taxes, leaving more money in the hands of consumers and businesses, encouraging spending and investment. Conversely, during periods of high inflation, a government might decrease spending or raise taxes to cool down the economy and curb rising prices. These levers, spending and taxation, are the core mechanisms of fiscal policy.

Monetary policy, on the other hand, is the purview of the central bank. Its primary goal is maintaining price stability, typically by controlling the money supply and interest rates. When inflation threatens, the central bank can raise interest rates, making borrowing more expensive. This slows down lending and investment, reducing the amount of money circulating and thus curbing inflation. Conversely, during a recession, the central bank might lower interest rates to stimulate borrowing and investment, encouraging economic activity and job growth. Open market operations, where the central bank buys or sells government bonds to influence the money supply, are another key tool in their arsenal.

The interaction between fiscal and monetary policy is where the real complexity lies. Imagine a scenario where the government is pursuing expansionary fiscal policy – increasing spending and cutting taxes – to combat a recession. Simultaneously, the central bank, concerned about potential inflation, tightens monetary policy by raising interest rates. These conflicting policies can create a push-pull effect, potentially neutralizing each other. The government's stimulus efforts are offset by the central bank's restrictive measures, leading to a muted impact on the economy.

Conversely, a well-coordinated approach can amplify the effectiveness of both policies. If both the government and central bank agree that stimulating the economy is necessary, they can work in tandem. The government's fiscal stimulus, combined with the central bank's low interest rates, creates a powerful synergy, accelerating economic recovery. This alignment of policies ensures that both are working towards the same goal, maximizing their impact.

The timing and magnitude of policy changes are also critical considerations. A delayed or insufficient response can exacerbate economic problems. For example, if the central bank waits too long to raise interest rates during an inflationary period, inflation can become entrenched, requiring even more drastic measures later on. Similarly, a premature tightening of fiscal policy can stifle a nascent recovery. Policymakers must carefully analyze economic data and anticipate future trends to make timely and appropriate adjustments.

The political environment also plays a significant role in the formulation and implementation of both fiscal and monetary policy. Government spending and taxation decisions are often influenced by political considerations, such as upcoming elections or the priorities of the ruling party. While central banks strive for independence, they are not entirely immune to political pressures. Understanding these political dynamics is crucial for interpreting policy decisions and their potential impact on the economy.

In addition, global economic conditions can significantly influence domestic policy decisions. A global recession, for instance, can constrain a country's ability to stimulate its own economy through fiscal policy. Similarly, fluctuations in exchange rates can impact the effectiveness of monetary policy. Policymakers must consider the global economic landscape and adjust their strategies accordingly. International coordination of fiscal and monetary policies can be crucial in addressing global economic challenges.

Furthermore, structural factors within an economy, such as labor market regulations and technological advancements, can impact the effectiveness of both fiscal and monetary policy. A rigid labor market, for example, can hinder the ability of monetary policy to stimulate employment. Policymakers must consider these structural factors when designing and implementing policies, adapting their strategies to the specific characteristics of their economy.

Finally, it's important to remember that economic forecasting is not an exact science. Unexpected events, such as natural disasters or geopolitical crises, can disrupt the best-laid plans. Policymakers must be prepared to adapt to changing circumstances and adjust their policies accordingly. Flexibility and responsiveness are essential qualities for effective economic management. A deep understanding of the complex interplay between fiscal and monetary policy, along with a nuanced appreciation for the various factors that influence their effectiveness, is essential for navigating the ever-evolving economic landscape.

3.4 International Trade

Navigating the complexities of international trade can feel like charting a course through uncharted waters. For newcomers, the sheer volume of information, regulations, and logistical hurdles can be overwhelming. This chapter aims to provide a practical roadmap, demystifying the process and equipping you with the knowledge to confidently engage in global commerce. We'll explore key concepts, delve into practical strategies, and highlight crucial considerations for success in the international marketplace.

Understanding the fundamental principles of international trade is paramount. It's not simply about buying and selling goods across borders; it's about navigating a complex interplay of economic forces, cultural nuances, and legal frameworks. A crucial first step is recognizing the comparative advantage your product or service offers. What makes your offering unique and desirable in the global market? Identifying your niche and understanding its potential within specific international markets is the cornerstone of a successful international trade strategy. This requires meticulous market research, including analyzing consumer demand, competitive landscapes, and existing trade agreements.

Once you've identified your target market, navigating the legal and regulatory landscape is essential. Each country has its own unique set of import and export regulations, tariffs, and customs procedures. Failure to comply with these regulations can lead to significant delays, penalties, and even legal repercussions. Thoroughly researching and understanding the specific requirements of your target market is crucial. Engaging with experienced customs brokers and international trade lawyers can provide invaluable guidance and ensure compliance, streamlining your entry into the global market. They can help you navigate complex documentation, tariff classifications, and other regulatory hurdles, saving you time and minimizing potential risks.

Logistics play a critical role in the success of international trade ventures. Efficient and reliable transportation of goods is essential. Consider the various shipping methods available, including sea freight, air freight, and rail transport, and choose the option that best balances cost, speed, and security for your specific product. Packaging and labeling requirements also vary significantly between countries. Ensure your products are packaged appropriately to withstand international shipping and comply with destination country regulations. Proper labeling, including accurate product descriptions, country of origin, and handling instructions, is crucial for customs clearance and efficient delivery.

Managing financial transactions in international trade requires careful planning and consideration. Currency fluctuations can significantly impact profitability, so understanding exchange rates and implementing strategies to mitigate currency risk is essential. Explore different payment methods, such as letters of credit, documentary collections, and wire transfers, and choose the option that best suits your business needs and minimizes risk. Building strong relationships with international banks experienced in facilitating global trade can provide valuable support and expertise.

Cultural sensitivity and effective communication are paramount in international trade. Understanding the cultural nuances of your target market is essential for building strong business relationships and ensuring successful transactions. Language barriers can present significant challenges, so investing in professional translation services for marketing materials, contracts, and other essential documents is crucial. Adapting your marketing messages and sales strategies to resonate with the cultural values and preferences of your target market can significantly enhance your chances of success.

Building strong relationships with international partners is a cornerstone of long-term success in global trade. Identifying reliable distributors, agents, or joint venture partners in your target market can provide invaluable local expertise and market access. Networking with industry associations and attending international trade shows can facilitate connections and open doors to new opportunities. Cultivating trust and mutual understanding with your international partners is essential for building sustainable and mutually beneficial relationships.

Managing risk is an inherent part of international trade. Political instability, economic downturns, and natural disasters can disrupt supply chains and impact profitability. Developing a comprehensive risk management plan is crucial for mitigating potential losses. Consider factors such as political risk insurance, cargo insurance, and contingency planning to protect your business from unforeseen events. Diversifying your markets and suppliers can also help minimize your exposure to risk.

Adaptability and continuous learning are essential for navigating the ever-evolving landscape of international trade. Global markets are dynamic, and regulations, consumer preferences, and competitive landscapes can change rapidly.

Staying informed about industry trends, attending relevant conferences and workshops, and engaging with industry experts can help you stay ahead of the curve and adapt your strategies accordingly. Embrace the challenges and view them as opportunities for growth and innovation.

Embarking on the journey of international trade can be both challenging and rewarding. By understanding the fundamental principles, navigating the legal and logistical complexities, and building strong international relationships, you can unlock the immense potential of the global marketplace and achieve lasting success. Remember that continuous learning, adaptability, and a commitment to cultural sensitivity are essential ingredients for thriving in the dynamic world of international trade.

3.5 Economic Development

Understanding economic development requires moving beyond simple measures of growth like Gross Domestic Product (GDP). While GDP provides a snapshot of a nation's economic output, it fails to capture the broader picture of societal well-being. True economic development encompasses improvements in living standards, reductions in poverty and inequality, and expansions in opportunities for individuals to reach their full potential. It's about creating an environment where people not only have more, but also live better, healthier, and more fulfilling lives. This requires a multi-faceted approach, considering factors beyond purely economic ones.

One crucial aspect of fostering economic development is investing in human capital. Education and skills training equip individuals with the tools they need to participate productively in the economy. A well-educated workforce is more adaptable to technological advancements, capable of innovation, and better positioned to secure higher-paying jobs. Furthermore, investments in healthcare are essential. A healthy population is more productive and can contribute more effectively to economic growth. Healthy individuals miss fewer workdays, experience higher levels of cognitive function, and are better equipped to handle the demands of a modern economy. These investments in human capital create a virtuous cycle, leading to a more skilled and productive workforce, which in turn drives further economic growth and development.

Infrastructure development plays a vital role in supporting economic activity. Reliable transportation networks, efficient energy systems, and robust communication infrastructure facilitate the movement of goods, services, and information. These networks connect businesses to markets, enable access to essential services, and promote regional integration. Consider the transformative impact of access to high-speed internet. It opens up opportunities for online education, remote work, and e-commerce, connecting previously isolated communities to the global economy. Investing in infrastructure not only boosts economic productivity but also enhances the quality of life for citizens by providing access to essential services and opportunities.

Promoting entrepreneurship and small business development is another key driver of economic development. Small and medium-sized enterprises (SMEs) are often the engines of job creation and innovation. They provide opportunities for individuals to start their own businesses, create employment for themselves and others, and contribute to the diversification of the economy. Governments can support SMEs through policies that streamline business registration processes, provide access to finance, and offer training and mentorship programs. A thriving entrepreneurial ecosystem fosters competition, drives innovation, and creates a more dynamic and resilient economy.

Creating a favorable business environment is crucial for attracting investment and promoting economic growth. This involves establishing clear and consistent regulations, ensuring property rights are protected, and minimizing bureaucratic hurdles. A predictable and transparent regulatory environment reduces uncertainty for businesses, encourages investment, and promotes long-term economic stability. Furthermore, a well-functioning legal system that enforces contracts and protects intellectual property is essential for fostering trust and encouraging innovation. When businesses feel confident that their investments are protected, they are more likely to take risks, expand their operations, and contribute to economic growth.

Fostering sustainable development is paramount for ensuring long-term economic prosperity. Economic development should not come at the expense of environmental degradation or social inequality. Sustainable development seeks to balance economic growth with environmental protection and social equity. This involves adopting environmentally friendly technologies, promoting responsible resource management, and investing in renewable energy sources. By prioritizing sustainable practices, we can ensure that future generations have the same opportunities for economic prosperity without compromising the health of the planet.

International trade and cooperation play a significant role in promoting economic development, particularly for developing countries. Access to global markets allows countries to specialize in the production of goods and services where they have a comparative advantage. This specialization leads to increased efficiency, higher output, and greater economic growth. Furthermore, international trade fosters the exchange of knowledge, technology, and ideas, which can further stimulate innovation and development. Participating in global trade agreements and engaging in international cooperation can provide developing countries with access to crucial resources, technical assistance, and market opportunities.

Good governance is essential for creating an environment conducive to economic development. Transparent and accountable institutions, effective public administration, and the rule of law are crucial for fostering trust, promoting investment, and ensuring efficient allocation of resources. Corruption, on the other hand, undermines economic development by diverting resources, distorting markets, and discouraging investment. Strengthening governance structures, promoting transparency, and combating corruption are essential for creating a level playing field for businesses and ensuring that public resources are used effectively to promote economic development.

Addressing inequality is critical for ensuring that the benefits of economic growth are shared broadly across society. High levels of inequality can lead to social unrest, undermine political stability, and hinder long-term economic growth. Policies that promote inclusive growth, such as investments in education, healthcare, and social safety nets, can help to reduce inequality and ensure that everyone has the opportunity to participate in and benefit from economic progress. A more equitable distribution of income and wealth not only improves social well-being but also strengthens the foundation for sustainable economic development.

By focusing on these multifaceted aspects, nations can move beyond simply measuring economic output and strive for true economic development that enhances the lives of their citizens. It's a long-term process that requires sustained effort, strategic planning, and a commitment to inclusive and sustainable growth. The ultimate goal is to create societies where everyone has the opportunity to thrive, reach their full potential, and live fulfilling lives.

4 Decoding Financial Markets

Financial markets are the lifeblood of any modern economy. They serve as vital conduits, channeling funds from those who have surplus capital (savers) to those who need it for investment (borrowers). This process of capital allocation is fundamental to economic growth, fostering innovation, creating jobs, and ultimately increasing overall societal wealth. Understanding their intricate workings is crucial for anyone seeking to navigate the complexities of the economic landscape. This intricate network facilitates the flow of funds, fostering economic growth and driving innovation.

At the heart of these markets lies a continuous interplay between supply and demand for capital. Think of it like any other market: the price of capital (represented by interest rates) is determined by the interaction of those seeking to borrow funds and those willing to lend. When the supply of capital is high, interest rates tend to be lower, encouraging businesses to invest and consumers to spend. Conversely, when capital is scarce, interest rates rise, dampening borrowing and spending. This dynamic equilibrium constantly adjusts to changes in economic conditions, influencing investment decisions and shaping the trajectory of economic activity. Factors like economic forecasts, investor confidence, and government policies all play a role in shaping this complex interplay.

Within this vast ecosystem, we encounter a variety of financial instruments, each with its own unique characteristics and purpose. These instruments can be broadly categorized into debt and equity, each representing a different way for entities to raise capital. Debt instruments, such as bonds, represent a loan made by an investor to a borrower (e.g., a corporation or government). Bondholders receive regular interest payments and the return of their principal at maturity. They are considered less risky than stocks but offer lower potential returns. The issuer is obligated to repay the principal plus interest, regardless of their financial performance.

Equity instruments, like stocks, represent ownership in a company. Stockholders become part-owners of the business and share in its profits (through dividends) and potential growth. However, they also bear the risk of the company's losses.

Stock prices fluctuate based on market sentiment, company performance, and broader economic factors. Unlike bondholders, stockholders have a claim on the company's assets but are last in line in the event of bankruptcy. Their returns are not guaranteed but have the potential to be significantly higher than bonds.

Adding another layer of complexity are derivatives, financial contracts whose value is derived from an underlying asset. These can include commodities, currencies, interest rates, or even other financial instruments like stocks and bonds. Derivatives serve various purposes, from hedging against risk to speculating on price movements. For example, a farmer might use a futures contract to lock in a price for their crops, protecting themselves against potential price declines. Similarly, a corporation might use a currency swap to mitigate the risk of exchange rate fluctuations. Understanding these complex instruments requires careful consideration of their inherent risks and potential rewards.

Navigating these markets effectively requires a deep understanding of various factors that influence their behavior. Macroeconomic indicators, such as inflation, unemployment, and economic growth, play a significant role. Changes in these indicators can impact investor sentiment, driving shifts in capital flows and influencing asset prices. For instance, rising inflation can erode the real returns of bonds, making them less attractive to investors. Similarly, strong economic growth can boost corporate earnings, leading to higher stock prices. Staying abreast of these macroeconomic trends is essential for making informed investment decisions.

Geopolitical events, both domestic and international, can also exert a powerful influence on financial markets. Political instability, trade wars, and natural disasters can all trigger market volatility. Investors react to these events based on their perceived impact on economic conditions and corporate profitability. For example, a trade war might negatively impact companies that rely heavily on international trade, leading to a decline in their stock prices. Keeping an eye on geopolitical developments is crucial for understanding potential market risks and opportunities.

Finally, investor psychology and market sentiment are significant drivers of market behavior. Fear, greed, and herd behavior can all lead to irrational market movements. During periods of market euphoria, investors may become overly optimistic, driving asset prices to unsustainable levels. Conversely, in times of fear and uncertainty, investors may panic sell, leading to sharp market declines. Understanding these psychological factors can help investors avoid making emotional decisions and maintain a disciplined investment approach. Recognizing the influence of market sentiment is essential for navigating the complexities of financial markets and making sound investment decisions. This involves critically evaluating market trends, avoiding herd mentality, and maintaining a long-term perspective on your investment goals. By considering these interconnected factors, individuals can gain a more comprehensive understanding of the dynamics driving financial markets and make more informed decisions to achieve their financial objectives.

4.1 The Role of Financial Markets

Understanding the role of financial markets is crucial for anyone navigating the world of finance. These markets serve as the vital link between those who have excess funds (savers or investors) and those who need funds (borrowers). They facilitate the efficient allocation of capital, driving economic growth and creating opportunities for individuals and businesses alike. Without functioning financial markets, businesses would struggle to secure financing for expansion, governments would face difficulties funding public services, and individuals would have fewer avenues for saving and investing. The intricate web of transactions within these markets determines interest rates, influences investment decisions, and ultimately shapes the economic landscape.

Financial markets encompass a wide range of venues where financial instruments like stocks, bonds, and currencies are traded. These markets can be broadly categorized into money markets, where short-term debt securities are traded, and capital markets, which deal in longer-term debt and equity instruments. Consider the money market as a place for short-term borrowing and lending, typically for less than a year. Businesses often utilize this market to manage their working capital needs, while governments use it to issue short-term debt instruments like Treasury bills. Conversely, the capital market is where companies raise long-term capital through the issuance of stocks and bonds. This market is crucial for funding long-term investments, such as building new factories or developing new technologies. The distinction between these two markets lies primarily in the maturity of the traded instruments, with the capital market providing the foundation for sustained economic growth.

Within capital markets, the stock market stands out as a significant component. Here, companies issue shares of ownership (stocks) to raise capital. Investors purchase these shares with the expectation of future returns through dividends or capital appreciation. Stock markets provide businesses with access to a vast pool of potential investors, enabling them to finance growth and innovation. Moreover, they offer individuals an opportunity to participate in the success of companies and build wealth over time. The performance of the stock market, often reflected in indices like the Dow Jones Industrial Average or the S&P 500, serves as a barometer of overall economic health. Fluctuations in stock prices reflect investor sentiment, economic prospects, and company performance, providing valuable insights into the state of the economy.

Bond markets, another crucial component of capital markets, facilitate the trade of debt securities. Governments and corporations issue bonds to borrow money from investors for a specific period, promising to repay the principal amount along with periodic interest payments. Bond markets provide a critical source of funding for public projects and corporate initiatives. They also offer investors a relatively stable income stream and a way to diversify their investment portfolios. The yields on bonds, representing the return an investor receives, are influenced by a range of factors, including prevailing interest rates, creditworthiness of the issuer, and overall market conditions.

Foreign exchange markets, often referred to as forex markets, facilitate the exchange of different currencies. This market is crucial for international trade and investment, enabling businesses to conduct transactions across borders and investors to allocate capital globally. The exchange rates between currencies are constantly fluctuating, influenced by factors such as interest rate differentials, economic growth prospects, and geopolitical events. Understanding these dynamics is essential for businesses engaged in international trade, as exchange rate fluctuations can significantly impact profitability.

Derivatives markets represent another complex yet important segment of financial markets. Derivatives are financial instruments whose value is derived from an underlying asset, such as a stock, bond, or commodity. These instruments include options, futures, and swaps, often used for hedging risks or speculating on price movements. While derivatives can be valuable tools for managing risk, their complexity and potential for high leverage can also pose significant risks if not used cautiously. Regulators play a vital role in overseeing these markets to ensure transparency and mitigate systemic risks.

The role of regulation in financial markets is paramount. Regulatory bodies, such as the Securities and Exchange Commission (SEC) in the United States, establish rules and regulations to protect investors, maintain market integrity, and prevent fraud. These regulations aim to ensure transparency, fair trading practices, and the dissemination of accurate information. Effective regulation promotes investor confidence, fosters market stability, and safeguards the overall financial system. Furthermore, regulations are crucial for preventing excessive risk-taking and mitigating the potential for financial crises.

Beyond these core market segments, the financial landscape encompasses other specialized markets, each serving a distinct purpose. Commodities markets, for example, facilitate the trade of raw materials like oil, gold, and agricultural products. These markets play a crucial role in determining the prices of essential commodities, impacting businesses and consumers alike. Real estate markets, where properties are bought and sold, are another significant component of the financial system, influencing economic growth and individual wealth accumulation. Understanding the interplay between these various markets provides a comprehensive perspective on the dynamics of the financial system.

The efficient functioning of financial markets relies on the availability of accurate and timely information. Transparency and information symmetry are essential for investors to make informed decisions and for markets to operate efficiently. When information is readily available and accessible to all market participants, it reduces the likelihood of market manipulation and promotes fair pricing. This transparency also fosters trust and confidence in the financial system, encouraging greater participation and contributing to economic growth.

Navigating the complexities of financial markets requires a solid understanding of their various components and their interconnectedness. Whether you are an individual investor, a business owner, or simply a concerned citizen, appreciating the role of financial markets is crucial for making informed financial decisions and understanding the broader economic landscape. By fostering financial literacy and promoting responsible financial practices, we can contribute to a more stable and prosperous financial system for all.

4.2 Stocks and Bonds

The world of finance can seem daunting, a labyrinth of jargon and complex instruments. However, at its core, investing is about putting your money to work for you, allowing it to grow over time. Two of the most fundamental investment vehicles are stocks and bonds. Understanding their distinct characteristics is crucial for building a diversified and successful portfolio.

Stocks represent ownership in a company. When you buy a stock, you become a shareholder, owning a small piece of that business. Your returns are tied to the company's performance. If the company thrives, its stock price typically increases, allowing you to sell your shares for a profit. Conversely, if the company struggles, the stock price may decline, leading to potential losses. Owning stock also gives you certain rights, such as voting on company matters. However, it's important to remember that stocks are considered riskier investments than bonds due to their price volatility. This volatility is influenced by a multitude of factors, from company-specific news and earnings reports to broader economic trends and market sentiment.

While stocks represent ownership, bonds represent debt. When you buy a bond, you are essentially lending money to a company or government. In return, they promise to pay you back the principal amount at a specified date, known as the maturity date. They also typically pay you periodic interest payments, known as coupons. Bonds are generally considered less risky than stocks because they offer a fixed income stream and a guaranteed return of principal (assuming the issuer doesn't default). However, this lower risk often comes with lower potential returns. Bond prices can also fluctuate, primarily due to changes in interest rates. When interest rates rise, bond prices tend to fall, and vice versa.

Diversifying your portfolio across both stocks and bonds is a cornerstone of prudent investing. This strategy, known as asset allocation, aims to balance risk and return. The specific mix of stocks and bonds will depend on your individual risk tolerance, financial goals, and time horizon. A younger investor with a longer time horizon might allocate a larger portion of their portfolio to stocks, seeking higher potential growth. Conversely, an investor nearing retirement might prefer a more conservative approach, with a greater emphasis on bonds to preserve capital.

Beyond the broad categories of stocks and bonds, there are numerous subcategories and variations within each. Stocks can be categorized by market capitalization (large-cap, midcap, small-cap), sector (technology, healthcare, financials), and investment style (growth, value). Bonds can be classified by issuer (government, corporate, municipal), maturity date (short-term, intermediate-term, long-term), and credit quality (investment grade, high-yield). Understanding these nuances is crucial for making informed investment decisions.

Thoroughly researching individual stocks and bonds before investing is paramount. For stocks, this involves analyzing the company's financials, understanding its business model, and assessing its competitive landscape. For bonds, it's essential to evaluate the creditworthiness of the issuer and the prevailing interest rate environment. Numerous resources are available to assist with this research, including financial news websites, company filings, and independent research reports.

Beyond individual security selection, you can also invest in stocks and bonds through mutual funds and exchange-traded funds (ETFs). These investment vehicles pool money from multiple investors to invest in a diversified portfolio of securities. They offer a convenient and cost-effective way to gain exposure to a broad range of assets without having to research and purchase individual stocks and bonds. ETFs and mutual funds are subject to management fees, so it's important to compare expense ratios when choosing among different options.

It's vital to approach investing with a long-term perspective and avoid impulsive decisions based on short-term market fluctuations. Market corrections and downturns are inevitable, but over the long run, the stock market has historically trended upwards. Maintaining a disciplined approach, adhering to your investment strategy, and staying informed about market conditions are essential for achieving your financial goals.

Remember, the information presented here is for educational purposes only and is not financial advice. Consult with a qualified financial advisor before making any investment decisions. They can help you develop a personalized investment strategy tailored to your specific financial situation and goals. Building a solid foundation of knowledge about stocks and bonds is the first step towards taking control of your financial future.

Understanding the interplay between risk and return is paramount in navigating the investment landscape. Higher potential returns typically come with higher risk, and vice versa. Stocks, with their potential for significant growth, also carry the risk of significant losses. Bonds, on the other hand, offer a more stable income stream but with lower potential returns. Balancing these competing forces is the key to building a portfolio that aligns with your individual risk tolerance and financial objectives.

Navigating the complexities of stocks and bonds can be challenging, but the potential rewards make the effort worthwhile. By building a diversified portfolio, conducting thorough research, and maintaining a long-term perspective, you can position yourself for financial success. Remember, investing is a journey, not a destination, and continuous learning is crucial for staying ahead of the curve.

4.3 Derivatives and Risk Management

The world of finance can feel like a labyrinth, filled with complex instruments and jargon. Derivatives, often perceived as particularly intricate, are powerful tools that can be used for both hedging risks and speculating on future price movements. Understanding their function and potential pitfalls is crucial for navigating today's markets. This chapter will delve into the core concepts of derivatives and how they can be integrated into a robust risk management strategy.

Derivatives derive their value from an underlying asset, such as a stock, bond, commodity, or even an interest rate. Think of them as a bet on the future price of something else. A simple example is a futures contract. Imagine a farmer who wants to lock in a price for their wheat harvest later in the year. They can sell a futures contract, obligating them to deliver a certain amount of wheat at a predetermined price on a specific date. This protects the farmer from a potential drop in wheat prices. Conversely, a baker could buy the same futures contract to protect themselves from a price increase. Both parties are using derivatives to manage their risk.

Options are another common type of derivative. They grant the holder the right, but not the obligation, to buy or sell an underlying asset at a specific price (the strike price) on or before a certain date. A call option gives the right to buy, while a put option gives the right to sell. Options provide flexibility, allowing investors to profit from price movements while limiting potential losses. For instance, an investor believing a stock price will rise could buy a call option. If the stock price surpasses the strike price, the option becomes profitable. If it doesn't, the investor only loses the premium paid for the option.

Swaps represent a third major category of derivatives. These are agreements between two parties to exchange cash flows based on different underlying assets. Interest rate swaps are a prime example. One party might agree to pay a fixed interest rate while receiving a floating rate from the other party. This can be used to manage interest rate risk, transforming a variable expense into a predictable one, or vice versa. Companies often use swaps to hedge against fluctuations in currency exchange rates or commodity prices.

Successfully integrating derivatives into a risk management strategy requires a thorough understanding of the underlying asset and the specific derivative being used. It's crucial to assess the potential risks and rewards, factoring in market volatility and your own risk tolerance. Over-reliance on derivatives can be dangerous, as witnessed during the 2008 financial crisis. Complex derivative products, misunderstood and mismanaged, played a significant role in the market collapse.

Diversification is a cornerstone of sound risk management. Don't put all your eggs in one basket, as the saying goes. Spread your investments across different asset classes, sectors, and geographical regions. This helps mitigate the impact of any single investment performing poorly. Derivatives can be used to further diversify your portfolio by providing exposure to asset classes you might not otherwise access.

Regularly monitoring your portfolio and adjusting your strategy as needed is essential. Markets are dynamic, and what worked yesterday might not work tomorrow. Stay informed about economic trends, industry news, and geopolitical events that could impact your investments. Utilize appropriate risk metrics, such as Value at Risk (VaR) and stress testing, to assess your portfolio's vulnerability to adverse market movements.

Effective risk management involves establishing clear objectives and constraints. What are your investment goals? What level of risk are you comfortable taking? How long is your investment horizon? Answering these questions will help you develop a strategy tailored to your specific needs. Don't be afraid to seek professional advice if you're unsure how to proceed. A qualified financial advisor can provide valuable insights and guidance.

Understanding the tax implications of derivatives is also crucial. Tax regulations can be complex and vary depending on the type of derivative and the jurisdiction. It's essential to consult with a tax professional to ensure you're complying with all applicable laws and minimizing your tax liability. Failing to do so can result in unexpected and potentially significant costs.

Finally, remember that risk management is an ongoing process, not a one-time event. Continuously review your strategy, adapt to changing market conditions, and remain disciplined in your approach. Derivatives can be valuable tools when used wisely, but they can also be dangerous if misused. By understanding the principles outlined in this chapter, you can navigate the complexities of derivatives and integrate them effectively into a comprehensive risk management plan. This knowledge will empower you to make informed decisions, protect your capital, and achieve your financial goals. Don't underestimate the importance of continuous learning and staying informed about the ever-evolving world of finance.

5 Behavioral Economics

Traditional economic theory often assumes that individuals act rationally, maximizing their own self-interest with perfect information. However, the burgeoning field of behavioral economics challenges these assumptions, demonstrating that human decision-making is often influenced by psychological factors and cognitive biases. We are not always the rational actors that traditional economic models portray. Our decisions, particularly in the realm of finance, are often swayed by emotions, heuristics, and social influences. Understanding these deviations from rationality is crucial for navigating the complexities of financial markets and making sound investment choices. This knowledge empowers us to recognize our own vulnerabilities and make more informed decisions.

Loss aversion, a key concept in prospect theory, describes the tendency for individuals to feel the pain of a loss more strongly than the pleasure of an equivalent gain. For example, the psychological impact of losing $100 is typically greater than the positive feeling of gaining $100. This asymmetry in how we perceive gains and losses can lead to risk aversion, even in situations where taking a calculated risk would be beneficial in the long run. Investors influenced by loss aversion might hold onto losing investments for too long, hoping to recover their losses, or avoid potentially profitable investments due to fear of potential short-term declines. Recognizing this bias allows us to evaluate investment opportunities more objectively, focusing on long-term potential rather than short-term fluctuations.

Overconfidence is another pervasive bias that affects financial decision-making. Individuals tend to overestimate their own abilities and the accuracy of their predictions. This can lead to excessive trading, taking on too much risk, and neglecting diversification. Overconfident investors may believe they can consistently outperform the market, leading them to make impulsive decisions based on gut feelings rather than thorough analysis. By cultivating humility and acknowledging the limitations of our own knowledge, we can mitigate the negative consequences of overconfidence. Seeking advice from trusted financial advisors and conducting thorough research before making investment decisions are crucial steps in overcoming this bias.

The anchoring bias describes the tendency to rely too heavily on the first piece of information received, even if that information is irrelevant or inaccurate. For instance, an investor might fixate on the initial price of a stock, using it as a reference point for all future price movements. This can lead to overvaluing or undervaluing the stock, hindering sound investment decisions. Being aware of the anchoring bias enables us to critically evaluate all available information, avoiding undue influence from initial impressions or irrelevant data. Objective analysis and a focus on fundamentals are essential for overcoming this bias.

Herding behavior, driven by social influences, can also lead to irrational investment decisions. Individuals often follow the crowd, mimicking the actions of others, even if those actions are not aligned with their own best interests. This can create market bubbles and crashes, as investors blindly follow trends without conducting independent research. Developing independent thinking and resisting the urge to follow the crowd are essential for making sound investment choices. Critical analysis and a focus on individual financial goals can help investors avoid the pitfalls of herding behavior.

Framing effects demonstrate how the way information is presented can influence our choices. For example, presenting an investment opportunity as having a 90% chance of success is more appealing than presenting the same opportunity as having a 10% chance of failure, even though the information is identical. Recognizing framing effects allows us to see through manipulative marketing tactics and focus on the underlying substance of investment opportunities. Objectively evaluating the potential risks and rewards, regardless of how they are presented, is critical for making informed decisions.

Nudging, a concept from behavioral economics, uses subtle changes in choice architecture to influence behavior without restricting options. For example, automatically enrolling employees in retirement savings plans, while allowing them to opt out, can significantly increase participation rates. This simple nudge leverages inertia and the status quo bias to encourage positive financial behavior. Understanding how nudges work can empower individuals to make better choices and improve their financial well-being. Similarly, setting clear financial goals and automating savings contributions can be powerful nudges towards achieving long-term financial security.

Financial literacy and education play a crucial role in mitigating the negative impact of cognitive biases and improving financial decision-making. By understanding basic financial concepts, individuals are better equipped to evaluate investment opportunities, manage risk, and make informed choices about their personal finances. Investing in financial education and seeking advice from qualified professionals are essential steps towards achieving financial well-being. Continuous learning and staying informed about market trends are crucial for navigating the complexities of the financial world. The psychology of investing encompasses a wide range of emotional and cognitive factors that influence our decisions. Fear, greed, and regret can all play a significant role in how we invest our money. Recognizing these emotional influences and developing strategies to manage them is crucial for making rational investment choices. Cultivating emotional discipline, developing a long-term investment strategy, and seeking professional advice can help investors navigate the emotional rollercoaster of the financial markets.

5.1 Cognitive Biases in Finance

We are constantly bombarded with information, from news headlines to social media feeds, and this deluge can significantly impact our financial decisions. Our brains, while remarkably complex, are prone to shortcuts, known as cognitive biases, that can lead us astray. These biases are not mere flaws; they are ingrained evolutionary mechanisms designed to simplify complex situations. Understanding these biases is crucial for navigating the financial world effectively. By recognizing them, we can begin to mitigate their influence and make more rational choices.

One of the most pervasive biases is confirmation bias. We tend to seek out and favor information that confirms our existing beliefs, while dismissing evidence to the contrary. Imagine you've invested in a particular stock. You're likely to gravitate towards positive news about the company, while downplaying or ignoring any negative reports. This can lead to overconfidence and prevent you from recognizing warning signs, potentially resulting in significant losses. To combat confirmation bias, actively seek out diverse perspectives and critically evaluate information, even if it contradicts your initial assumptions. Consider the source's credibility and potential motivations. Challenging your own beliefs is a crucial step in making informed financial decisions.

Another common bias is the anchoring effect. This occurs when we rely too heavily on the first piece of information we receive, even if it's irrelevant. For example, if you see a car advertised at a heavily discounted price, that initial price becomes your anchor. Even if the original price was inflated, the discount will seem appealing. In investing, anchoring can lead to poor decisions, such as buying a stock simply because it has dropped significantly from its previous high, without considering the underlying reasons for the decline. To counteract the anchoring effect, research thoroughly and consider multiple factors before making a decision. Don't let the first piece of information you encounter unduly influence your judgment.

The availability heuristic is another significant bias that influences our financial choices. We tend to overestimate the likelihood of events that are easily recalled, often due to their vividness or recent occurrence. A market crash, for example, can leave a lasting impression, leading investors to overestimate the probability of another crash occurring soon. This can lead to risk aversion and missed investment opportunities. To mitigate the availability heuristic, focus on long-term trends and statistical data rather than relying on emotionally charged memories or anecdotal evidence. Diversification can also help manage risk and reduce the impact of unexpected events.

Loss aversion is a powerful bias that drives many financial

decisions. The pain of losing money is typically felt more strongly than the pleasure of gaining an equivalent amount. This can lead to risk-averse behavior, such as holding onto losing investments for too long in the hope of recovering losses, or avoiding potentially profitable investments due to fear of potential losses. Understanding loss aversion can help you make more rational choices by focusing on the overall potential return of an investment rather than fixating on potential losses. Establish clear investment goals and risk tolerance levels to guide your decision-making process.

The bandwagon effect describes our tendency to follow the crowd, even if it goes against our better judgment. This can be particularly dangerous in investing, as market bubbles often form due to herd mentality. When everyone is investing in a particular asset, it can create a sense of FOMO (fear of missing out), leading to irrational decisions. To avoid falling prey to the bandwagon effect, conduct independent research and make investment decisions based on your own analysis and goals. Don't be swayed by popular opinion or market hype.

Overconfidence bias can also lead to poor financial outcomes. We tend to overestimate our own abilities and knowledge, which can lead to excessive risk-taking and inadequate diversification. For example, an overconfident investor might concentrate their portfolio in a few stocks, believing they can accurately predict market movements. This can expose them to significant losses if their predictions prove incorrect. Recognize that markets are inherently unpredictable and that even experienced professionals make mistakes. Diversify your investments and seek professional advice when needed.

The framing effect demonstrates how the way information is presented can influence our decisions. For example, a product advertised as 90% fat-free seems more appealing than one labeled as 10% fat, even though they are identical. In finance, framing can influence how we perceive investment opportunities. A potential gain framed as a "sure thing" can seem more attractive than a statistically equivalent opportunity framed as a gamble, even though the expected return is the same. Be aware of how framing can manipulate your perceptions and focus on the underlying facts and figures when making financial decisions.

Finally, the sunk cost fallacy can trap us in poor investments. We tend to continue investing in something (time, money, or effort) simply because we have already invested in it, even if it's no longer rational to do so. For example, you might continue holding onto a losing stock because you've already invested a significant amount of money in it. Recognize that past investments are sunk costs and should not influence your future decisions. Be willing to cut your losses and move on to more promising opportunities.

By understanding and acknowledging these cognitive biases, you can significantly improve your financial decision-making. Remember that these biases are inherent to human nature, and even the most experienced investors are susceptible to them. The key is to be aware of their influence and actively work to mitigate their impact. By developing a disciplined and rational approach to investing, you can navigate the complexities of the financial world with greater confidence and success.

5.2 Prospect Theory and Loss Aversion

Imagine walking into a casino. You're handed two options: a guaranteed $50, or a 50% chance of winning $100 and a 50% chance of winning nothing. Most people choose the sure $50, even though mathematically the expected value of both options is the same. This seemingly irrational preference reveals a fundamental principle of behavioral economics: we feel the pain of a loss more strongly than the pleasure of an equivalent gain. This is the core of loss aversion, a critical component of prospect theory.

Loss aversion isn't just about gambling. It influences our decisions in every area of life, from investing to negotiating salaries to choosing a health plan. Consider two health plans: one emphasizes the 90% survival rate of a particular surgery, while the other highlights the 10% mortality rate. While statistically equivalent, the framing drastically affects our perception. We are drawn to the plan highlighting survival, instinctively recoiling from the one emphasizing potential loss. This emotional response, driven by loss aversion, often leads us to make choices that aren't statistically optimal, yet feel safer. Understanding this bias can help us make more rational decisions.

Prospect theory, developed by Daniel Kahneman and Amos Tversky, provides a framework for understanding how people make decisions under conditions of risk and uncertainty. It builds upon traditional economic models, but incorporates psychological factors like loss aversion. The theory posits that we don't evaluate outcomes based on absolute wealth, but rather on changes relative to a reference point. This reference point can be our current situation, our expectations, or even the status of others. A gain of $100 feels significant to someone with $1,000 in savings but less so to someone with $1 million.

Similarly, a loss of $100 impacts the person with less savings more severely.

The asymmetry between gains and losses explains why we are often risk-averse when it comes to potential gains, preferring a sure thing over a gamble with a higher expected value. Conversely, when faced with potential losses, we become risk-seeking, hoping to avoid the loss altogether even if it means taking a gamble with a lower expected value. This is why people sometimes hold onto losing investments for too long, hoping they will rebound, even when the rational choice would be to cut their losses. They feel the pain of selling at a loss more acutely than the potential future losses of holding onto a declining asset.

The concept of the "value function" in prospect theory illustrates this asymmetry. The value function is steeper for losses than for gains, visually representing the greater impact of losses on our decision-making. A small loss has a disproportionately large negative impact on our perceived value, while a small gain has a relatively smaller positive impact. This difference in slope explains our tendency to overweight losses and underweight gains. Consider a negotiation scenario. A concession feels like a loss, and we fight harder to avoid it, even if it means sacrificing a potentially larger gain. Understanding this dynamic can help us negotiate more effectively. Another key aspect of prospect theory is the concept of "probability weighting." We don't treat probabilities objectively. We tend to overweight small probabilities and underweight large probabilities. This explains the appeal of lotteries, where the minuscule chance of a huge win is overweighted, making the gamble seem more attractive than it is statistically. Similarly, we often underweight the high probability of smaller, more frequent events, leading to inadequate preparation for common risks. Think about insurance. We are willing to pay premiums to protect against low-probability, high-impact events like house fires, even though the likelihood of such an event is relatively small.

Loss aversion and probability weighting combine to create powerful biases in our decision-making. Recognizing these biases is the first step towards mitigating their influence. By consciously acknowledging our tendency to overweight losses and small probabilities, we can make more rational choices. When evaluating options, try to frame them in terms of both gains and losses. Consider the potential downsides of avoiding a loss, and the potential upsides of accepting a smaller, more certain gain.

Furthermore, try to evaluate probabilities objectively. Don't

be swayed by the allure of small probabilities of large gains, or the complacency induced by high probabilities of small losses. Research and understand the actual statistical likelihood of different outcomes. By taking a more analytical approach, we can overcome the emotional pull of loss aversion and make decisions based on logic and reason.
Finally, consider the concept of "mental accounting." We tend to categorize and treat money differently depending on its source and intended use. Money earned through hard work is often valued more highly than money won in a lottery. This can lead to irrational spending patterns. By recognizing that money is fungible, regardless of its origin, we can make more consistent and rational financial decisions. Understanding how prospect theory influences our choices empowers us to make better decisions in all aspects of our lives, from our finances to our health to our relationships. By acknowledging and mitigating our biases, we can navigate the complex world of decision-making with greater clarity and confidence.

5.3 Nudging and Choice Architecture

We're constantly making choices. From the mundane – what to have for breakfast – to the life-altering – which career path to pursue – our days are filled with decisions. What we often fail to realize is how subtly these choices are influenced by the environment around us. This "environment" isn't just the physical space, but also the way information is presented, the default options available, and the social norms we perceive. This is the realm of choice architecture and nudging.

Think about the last time you were in a cafeteria. Were the healthier options placed at eye level, or tucked away in a corner? Was the dessert display prominently featured? These seemingly small details are examples of choice architecture: the deliberate design of environments to influence decision-making. By understanding the principles of choice architecture, we can make better choices for ourselves and create environments that encourage others to do the same.

Nudging is a specific type of choice architecture that gently guides people towards desirable behaviors without restricting their freedom of choice. It's about making the healthy choice the easy choice. For example, automatically enrolling employees in a retirement savings plan (with the option to opt-out) is a nudge. It encourages saving without forcing anyone to participate. Similarly, placing fruit at the checkout counter instead of candy is a nudge that can promote healthier snacking habits. These subtle interventions can have a significant impact on individual and collective well-being.

The power of nudges lies in their ability to leverage human psychology. We are often influenced by cognitive biases – predictable patterns of irrationality in our thinking. One such bias is the "default effect," which refers to our tendency to stick with the pre-selected option. This explains why automatic enrollment in retirement plans is so effective. Changing the default requires effort, and most people simply go with the flow.

Another key principle is "loss aversion." We feel the pain of a loss more strongly than the pleasure of an equivalent gain. Framing a choice in terms of what we stand to lose can be a powerful motivator. For instance, highlighting the potential health risks of smoking (loss of health) is often more effective than emphasizing the benefits of quitting (gaining health).

Social proof also plays a significant role in our decisions. We tend to follow the crowd, especially when we're unsure what to do. If we see that most people in our community recycle, we're more likely to recycle ourselves. Highlighting the positive behaviors of others can be a powerful nudge.

Designing effective nudges requires careful consideration of the context. What works in one situation may not work in another. For example, while automatic enrollment in retirement plans is effective for many, it might not be appropriate for individuals facing financial hardship. It's crucial to consider the potential downsides of any nudge and ensure that it doesn't disproportionately impact vulnerable populations.

Ethical considerations are also paramount. Nudging should always be transparent and respect individual autonomy. People should be aware that they are being nudged and have the freedom to choose differently. Manipulative tactics that exploit vulnerabilities or deceive individuals are never acceptable.

Applying these principles in our own lives can lead to significant improvements in our decision-making. Start by becoming aware of your own biases. Are you susceptible to the default effect? Do you tend to overestimate your abilities? Once you understand your own tendencies, you can take steps to mitigate their influence.

Creating a supportive environment is also crucial. Organize your physical space to promote healthy habits. If you want to eat healthier, make sure healthy foods are readily available and visible. If you want to exercise more, keep your workout clothes in a convenient location. Small changes in your environment can make a big difference in your behavior.

Finally, remember that change takes time and effort. Don't get discouraged if you don't see results immediately. Be patient with yourself and keep experimenting with different nudges until you find what works best for you. By understanding the principles of choice architecture and nudging, you can empower yourself to make better choices and create a more fulfilling life. The small, deliberate changes you make today can have a profound impact on your future. Embrace the power of nudges and unlock your potential for positive change. Start small, stay consistent, and watch as your choices lead you towards a brighter tomorrow. The journey may not always be easy, but the rewards are well worth the effort. Take control of your choices and shape your destiny, one nudge at a time.

5.4 Financial Literacy and Education

Understanding your financial situation is the cornerstone of a secure future. This doesn't require a degree in economics, but rather a willingness to engage with your finances actively. It's about taking control of your money, not letting it control you. Start by meticulously tracking your income and expenses. Every penny earned and spent should be accounted for. Use budgeting apps, spreadsheets, or even a simple notebook. The goal is to create a clear picture of your cash flow, identifying where your money is coming from and where it's going. This awareness is fundamental to making informed financial decisions.

Once you have a handle on your cash flow, the next crucial step is budgeting. A budget isn't about restriction; it's about empowerment. It's a roadmap for your money, guiding you toward your financial goals. Allocate your income towards essential expenses like housing, food, and transportation. Then, factor in savings and debt repayment. Consider the 50/30/20 rule: 50% of your income for needs, 30% for wants, and 20% for savings and debt repayment. This is a guideline, adjust it to suit your individual circumstances. The key is to create a sustainable budget that aligns with your values and aspirations. Regularly review and revise your budget as needed, adapting it to life's changes.

Saving is the bedrock of financial security. It provides a cushion for unexpected expenses, allows you to pursue opportunities, and builds a foundation for future goals. Aim to build an emergency fund covering 3-6 months of essential living expenses. This fund provides a safety net in times of job loss, unexpected medical bills, or other emergencies. Beyond the emergency fund, save for specific goals like a down payment on a house, a car, or retirement. Explore different savings vehicles, such as high-yield savings accounts, money market accounts, and certificates of deposit (CDs). Consider the interest rates, accessibility, and risk factors associated with each option.

Managing debt effectively is crucial for financial health. High-interest debt can quickly erode your financial progress. Prioritize paying down high-interest debt, such as credit card balances, as quickly as possible. Explore strategies like the debt snowball or debt avalanche methods to accelerate debt repayment. The debt snowball method focuses on paying off the smallest debt first, while the debt avalanche method prioritizes the debt with the highest interest rate. Choose the strategy that best motivates you and fits your financial situation. While managing existing debt, avoid accumulating new debt whenever possible.

Investing is a powerful tool for building long-term wealth. It allows your money to grow over time, outpacing inflation and increasing your purchasing power. Start by understanding your risk tolerance and investment timeline. If you're investing for retirement decades away, you can typically tolerate more risk than someone investing for a short-term goal. Diversify your investments across different asset classes, such as stocks, bonds, and real estate. Diversification helps mitigate risk by spreading your investments across different sectors and asset types. Consider investing in low-cost index funds or exchange-traded funds (ETFs) for broad market exposure.

Protecting your assets is essential to safeguarding your financial well-being. Insurance provides a safety net against unforeseen events, mitigating potential financial losses. Evaluate your insurance needs, including health insurance, auto insurance, homeowners or renters insurance, and life insurance. Health insurance protects you from potentially devastating medical expenses. Auto insurance covers liability and damages in case of an accident. Homeowners or renters insurance protects your belongings and provides liability coverage. Life insurance provides financial support for your dependents in the event of your death.

Planning for retirement is a crucial long-term financial goal. Start saving for retirement as early as possible to take advantage of the power of compounding. Contribute to employer-sponsored retirement plans, such as 401(k)s or 403(b)s, especially if your employer offers matching contributions. Consider opening an Individual Retirement Account (IRA) to supplement your retirement savings. Explore different investment options within your retirement accounts, balancing risk and potential return based on your time horizon.

Building a good credit score is essential for accessing favorable financial products and services. A strong credit score can help you secure lower interest rates on loans, qualify for better credit card offers, and even rent an apartment. Pay your bills on time, every time. Keep your credit utilization low, ideally below 30% of your available credit. Monitor your credit reports regularly for errors and discrepancies. Building and maintaining a good credit score requires consistent responsible financial behavior.

Seeking professional financial advice can provide valuable guidance and support in navigating complex financial matters. A financial advisor can help you develop a personalized financial plan, manage investments, and plan for retirement. When choosing a financial advisor, consider their qualifications, experience, and fee structure. Ensure they are a fiduciary, meaning they are legally obligated to act in your best interest.

Continuously educating yourself about personal finance is crucial for making informed decisions and achieving your financial goals. Stay informed about financial news and trends. Read books, articles, and blogs on personal finance topics. Attend workshops or webinars on financial literacy. The more you learn about managing your finances, the better equipped you'll be to make sound financial choices. Embrace lifelong learning as a path to financial empowerment.

5.5 The Psychology of Investing

Fear and greed. These two primal emotions are the twin engines driving market behavior, and understanding their influence is crucial for any investor. While seemingly simple, their impact on our decision-making process is profound, often leading us to buy high and sell low, the exact opposite of what we should be doing. Recognize these emotions in yourself. Acknowledge their presence. This awareness alone can significantly improve your investment outcomes. Don't fight them; instead, learn to manage them.
Consider the concept of "loss aversion." Studies have shown that the pain of a loss is psychologically twice as powerful as the pleasure of an equivalent gain. This inherent bias can make investors overly cautious, clinging to losing positions in the hope of breaking even, while simultaneously selling winning investments prematurely to lock in small profits. Understanding loss aversion helps us appreciate why we sometimes make irrational decisions. It allows us to create strategies to mitigate its impact, such as setting predefined stop-loss or-

ders and taking profits at predetermined levels. These strategies, based on logic rather than emotion, can help protect your portfolio from the whims of the market.

Another critical aspect of investment psychology is "confirmation bias." This is our tendency to seek out and favor information that confirms our existing beliefs, while dismissing information that contradicts them. We see what we want to see. Imagine you've invested in a particular company. You're likely to pay more attention to positive news articles about that company while ignoring any negative press. This selective filtering can lead to overconfidence and prevent us from recognizing warning signs. Challenge your assumptions. Actively seek out dissenting viewpoints. This practice can help you make more objective and informed investment decisions.

The "bandwagon effect" plays a significant role in market bubbles and crashes. This is the phenomenon where people adopt beliefs and behaviors because many other people are doing so. It's the herd mentality at play in the financial markets. When everyone is buying a particular stock or asset class, it creates a sense of FOMO (fear of missing out), driving prices up to unsustainable levels. Conversely, when the market turns, this same herd mentality can lead to panic selling, driving prices down even further. Recognize the power of the crowd. Don't blindly follow trends. Develop your own independent investment strategy based on sound fundamentals.

"Anchoring bias" is another cognitive trap to be aware of. This occurs when we rely too heavily on the first piece of information we receive, even if it's irrelevant. For example, if you first heard about a stock when it was trading at $100, you might consider it expensive at $150, even if its intrinsic value is actually much higher. This initial "anchor" can influence our perception of value, preventing us from recognizing good investment opportunities. Be mindful of the information you consume. Question your assumptions about value. Conduct thorough research to determine the true worth of an investment.

Overconfidence can also lead to poor investment decisions. We tend to overestimate our abilities and underestimate the role of luck. This can lead to excessive trading, concentrated portfolios, and ultimately, lower returns. Humility is essential in investing. Acknowledge your limitations. Diversify your portfolio to reduce risk. Remember that even the most experienced investors make mistakes.

Patience is a virtue, especially in investing. The desire for quick profits can lead to impulsive decisions and chasing short-term gains. Building wealth takes time and discipline.

Focus on long-term growth. Avoid market timing. Stay the course.

The market is a complex and unpredictable beast. External factors, such as economic news, political events, and natural disasters, can all impact market performance. Accept that you cannot control everything. Develop a robust investment strategy that can withstand market fluctuations. Don't panic sell during market downturns. Instead, view these periods as opportunities to buy quality assets at discounted prices.

Successful investing requires more than just financial knowledge. It also requires an understanding of human psychology and the biases that can influence our decisions. By recognizing these biases and developing strategies to mitigate their impact, you can improve your investment outcomes and achieve your financial goals. Remember, investing is a marathon, not a sprint.

Finally, understand your own risk tolerance. How much volatility can you comfortably handle? Your risk tolerance will depend on factors such as your age, financial goals, and personal circumstances. Don't invest in assets that keep you up at night. Choose investments that align with your risk profile and investment horizon. A well-diversified portfolio tailored to your individual needs is the cornerstone of sound financial planning. Stay informed, stay disciplined, and stay focused on your long-term goals.

6 The Global Economy

The world economy isn't a collection of isolated entities, but a complex web of interconnected relationships. National economies are increasingly intertwined through trade, capital flows, migration, and the sharing of technology and information. Understanding this interconnectedness, or globalization, is crucial to navigating the complexities of international finance. This intricate system creates a dynamic where events in one country can ripple across borders, impacting other nations in sometimes unexpected ways. Consider, for example, how a change in interest rates by the Federal Reserve in the United States can influence investment decisions in emerging markets. Or how a supply chain disruption in Asia can lead to shortages and price increases in Europe and North America. This interdependence necessitates a global perspective when analyzing economic trends and formulating policy responses. International financial institutions play a pivotal role in shaping the global economic landscape. Organizations like the International Monetary Fund (IMF), the World Bank, and the World Trade Organization (WTO) provide a framework for international cooperation and coordination. The IMF, for instance, works to stabilize exchange rates and provide financial assistance to countries facing balance-of-payments crises. Its lending programs often come with conditions aimed at promoting structural reforms and sound economic policies. The World Bank, on the other hand, focuses on promoting long-term economic development by providing loans and grants for infrastructure projects, education, and healthcare in developing countries. Its goal is to reduce poverty and improve living standards. The WTO aims to liberalize trade by reducing tariffs and other barriers, facilitating the smooth flow of goods and services across borders. It also provides a forum for resolving trade disputes between nations. These institutions, while sometimes criticized for their policies and influence, are nonetheless essential components of the global economic architecture.

Emerging markets represent a significant and rapidly evolving force in the global economy. Characterized by rapid growth, increasing industrialization, and evolving institutional frameworks, these economies present both immense opportunities and unique challenges. Countries like China, India, Brazil, and Indonesia have become major players in international trade and investment. Their growing middle classes represent a substantial market for goods and services, attracting foreign investment and driving global demand. However, emerging markets also face significant hurdles, including infrastructure gaps, institutional weaknesses, and vulnerability to external shocks. These challenges underscore the importance of sustainable development strategies that promote inclusive growth and address social and environmental concerns. Investing in education, healthcare, and infrastructure, as well as fostering good governance and transparency, is crucial for unleashing the full potential of these dynamic economies.

Navigating the complexities of the global economy requires understanding the interplay between globalization, international institutions, and the unique dynamics of emerging markets. The interconnectedness of national economies through trade and finance creates both opportunities and vulnerabilities. Opportunities arise from access to larger markets, greater specialization, and the potential for faster economic growth. However, this interconnectedness also exposes countries to the risks of contagion, where economic shocks in one region can quickly spread to others. The 2008 financial crisis, for example, vividly demonstrated how interconnectedness can amplify the impact of a crisis. The collapse of the U.S. housing market triggered a chain reaction that quickly spread across the globe, leading to a worldwide recession.

International financial institutions play a crucial role in mitigating these risks and promoting global economic stability. By providing financial assistance, promoting policy coordination, and facilitating dialogue, these institutions help to manage crises and foster sustainable development. They also play a key role in setting international standards and regulations, promoting transparency, and combating corruption. Their effectiveness, however, depends on the cooperation and commitment of member countries, as well as their ability to adapt to evolving global challenges.

Emerging markets, with their dynamic growth and increasing integration into the global economy, present a complex set of opportunities and challenges. Their rapid economic expansion offers significant potential for investors and businesses, while also posing risks associated with political instability, regulatory uncertainty, and volatile markets. Understanding the specific characteristics of each emerging market, its strengths and weaknesses, is essential for successful engagement. This requires careful analysis of economic indicators, political developments, and social trends. It also necessitates a long-term perspective and a willingness to navigate the complexities of these dynamic economies.

Global economic governance is a continuous process of adaptation and reform. The evolving landscape of the world economy, with its increasing complexity and interconnectedness, requires ongoing efforts to strengthen international cooperation, improve regulatory frameworks, and promote sustainable development. This includes addressing issues such as climate change, income inequality, and technological disruption. The future of the global economy depends on the ability of nations and international institutions to work together to manage these challenges and create a more inclusive and sustainable economic system. This collaborative effort requires not only effective policies and institutions but also a shared vision for a prosperous and equitable future.

6.1 Globalization and Interdependence

We live in a world stitched together by invisible threads of trade, communication, and shared challenges. This interconnectedness, what we call globalization, isn't a recent invention. For centuries, humans have exchanged goods, ideas, and cultures. Think of the Silk Road, a network of trade routes that connected the East and West, fostering the exchange of everything from silk and spices to religion and philosophy. However, the pace and scale of globalization today are unprecedented, driven by technological advancements, reduced trade barriers, and increased international cooperation. This intricate web of relationships has created a world where events in one corner can ripple across the globe, impacting economies, environments, and societies far removed from the initial point of origin.

Consider the global supply chains that bring us our everyday products. A smartphone, for instance, might contain components manufactured in multiple countries, assembled in another, and then shipped worldwide. This intricate dance of production highlights the deep interdependence that characterizes our globalized world. A disruption in one part of this chain, whether due to political instability, natural disasters, or even a pandemic, can send shockwaves through the entire system, leading to shortages, price hikes, and economic instability. This level of interconnectedness presents both immense opportunities and significant challenges, requiring a nuanced understanding of the forces at play.

One of the most significant benefits of globalization is increased economic growth. By opening up to international trade, countries can specialize in producing goods and services where they have a comparative advantage. This specialization leads to greater efficiency, lower costs, and increased overall output. Developing countries, in particular, have benefited from access to global markets, allowing them to attract foreign investment, create jobs, and improve living standards. However, this economic integration isn't without its drawbacks. It can also lead to increased income inequality within countries, as the benefits of globalization are not always evenly distributed.

Beyond economics, globalization has profoundly impacted culture and communication. The spread of information and ideas through the internet and social media has fostered greater cultural exchange and understanding. We can now access news, entertainment, and educational resources from around the world, exposing us to diverse perspectives and enriching our understanding of different cultures. However, this increased connectivity also raises concerns about cultural homogenization, the loss of local traditions, and the potential for misinformation and manipulation. Maintaining a balance between embracing global interconnectedness and preserving cultural diversity is a crucial challenge in our increasingly globalized world.

The environment is another arena where the effects of globalization are deeply felt. Increased economic activity and global trade have led to increased pollution and resource depletion. The interconnected nature of ecosystems means that environmental problems, such as climate change and deforestation, transcend national borders and require international cooperation to address effectively. The globalization of environmental challenges necessitates a shift towards global governance and collaborative solutions, recognizing that the health of our planet is a shared responsibility.

Political systems have also been reshaped by the forces of globalization. International organizations, such as the United Nations and the World Trade Organization, have emerged to address global issues and facilitate cooperation between nations. The rise of multinational corporations has also shifted the balance of power, with some corporations wielding significant influence over national governments. Navigating the complex interplay between national sovereignty and global governance is a key challenge in the 21st century.

Globalization also presents ethical dilemmas. Issues such as fair trade, labor standards, and human rights have taken on a global dimension. The interconnectedness of our world requires us to consider the ethical implications of our consumption choices and the impact of our actions on people and communities across the globe. Promoting ethical behavior in a globalized world requires international cooperation, transparency, and a commitment to social responsibility.

Understanding the dynamics of globalization is essential for navigating the complexities of the modern world. It requires a nuanced understanding of the economic, political, cultural, and environmental forces at play. By recognizing the interconnectedness of our world and embracing the opportunities while addressing the challenges, we can harness the power of globalization to create a more just, prosperous, and sustainable future for all. This involves fostering cross-cultural understanding, promoting sustainable development, and strengthening international cooperation.

Moving forward, we must prioritize equitable and sustainable globalization, ensuring that its benefits are shared more widely and that its negative impacts are mitigated. This requires a shift towards a more inclusive and collaborative approach to global governance, one that prioritizes the well-being of all people and the health of our planet. Education and awareness are crucial in fostering a global citizenry equipped to navigate the complexities of our interconnected world.

The challenges of globalization are significant, but so are the opportunities. By embracing a spirit of cooperation and working together to address shared challenges, we can harness the power of globalization to create a better future for all. This requires a commitment to building bridges of understanding, fostering sustainable development, and promoting a more just and equitable world. The future of globalization rests on our ability to embrace our shared humanity and work together to build a more interconnected and prosperous world.

6.2 International Financial Institutions

The global financial landscape is a complex web of interconnected institutions, agreements, and regulations. Navigating this terrain can feel daunting, but understanding the key players—specifically international financial institutions—is crucial for anyone seeking to engage with the global economy. These institutions, often operating across borders and impacting economies worldwide, play a significant role in shaping financial stability, promoting development, and facilitating international trade. They offer valuable resources and expertise but also present unique challenges and considerations.

The International Monetary Fund (IMF), often seen as the global lender of last resort, provides financial assistance to countries experiencing balance of payments problems. These loans are typically conditional, requiring recipient nations to implement specific economic reforms aimed at addressing the root causes of their financial instability. The IMF also monitors global economic trends, publishes data and analysis, and offers technical assistance to its member countries. Understanding the IMF's role and the implications of its lending practices is crucial for grasping the dynamics of international finance. Its influence extends beyond individual nations, affecting global financial stability and the flow of capital across borders.

The World Bank Group, comprised of several distinct institutions, focuses on promoting long-term economic development and poverty reduction. Through providing loans, grants, and technical assistance, the World Bank supports a wide range of projects in developing countries, from infrastructure development and education to health initiatives and environmental protection. Each institution within the World Bank Group has a specialized focus, addressing specific development challenges. For instance, the International Development Association (IDA) provides concessional loans and grants to the poorest countries, while the International Finance Corporation (IFC) promotes private sector investment in developing economies. Navigating the complexities of the World Bank Group requires understanding its diverse components and their individual roles.

Regional development banks, like the Asian Development Bank, the African Development Bank, the Inter-American Development Bank, and the European Bank for Reconstruction and Development, play a crucial role in financing development within specific geographic regions. They often possess in-depth knowledge of the unique challenges and opportunities within their respective regions, allowing them to tailor their interventions more effectively. These banks not only provide financial resources but also offer technical expertise and promote regional cooperation on development initiatives. Understanding their individual mandates and areas of focus provides a deeper understanding of regional economic dynamics.

Beyond these prominent multilateral institutions, bilateral development banks also play a significant role in international finance. These institutions, typically owned by a single country, focus on providing development assistance to specific partner countries. While their operations may be smaller in scale compared to multilateral institutions, their targeted approach often allows for a more direct and tailored impact. Analyzing the strategies and priorities of bilateral development banks offers insights into the development agendas of individual nations and their relationships with partner countries.

Export-Import Banks, commonly known as EXIM banks, are government agencies that facilitate international trade by providing financing and insurance to exporters and importers. These institutions help businesses mitigate the risks associated with international trade and access financing that may not be readily available from commercial banks. Understanding the role of EXIM banks is crucial for businesses engaged in international trade, as they can provide valuable support for navigating the complexities of exporting and importing goods and services.

The Bank for International Settlements (BIS), often called the "central bank of central banks," fosters international monetary and financial cooperation among central banks and other international financial institutions. It serves as a forum for discussion and collaboration on issues related to financial stability, regulatory frameworks, and international payments systems. The BIS's role in promoting dialogue and coordination among central banks is critical for maintaining a stable and well-functioning global financial system. Understanding its functions offers insight into the inner workings of international financial cooperation and the efforts to mitigate systemic risks.

In addition to these institutions, numerous international organizations play a supportive role in shaping the global financial landscape. Organizations like the World Trade Organization (WTO), the Organization for Economic Co-operation and Development (OECD), and the G20, though not strictly financial institutions, influence international financial policies and regulations. Their work impacts trade, investment, and financial flows, creating a complex interplay between economic and financial policies. Understanding these connections is vital for navigating the broader context of international finance.

Navigating the complexities of international finance requires not only understanding the individual roles of these institutions but also recognizing their interconnectedness. These institutions often collaborate and coordinate their efforts, creating a web of influence that shapes global financial markets and development outcomes. Understanding the interplay between these institutions is essential for effectively engaging with the international financial system. Furthermore, critical evaluation of their practices and policies is essential for promoting a more just and sustainable global economy.

Analyzing the impact of these institutions, both individually and collectively, is crucial for understanding the flow of capital, the dynamics of development, and the evolution of the global financial architecture. These organizations are not static entities; they adapt and evolve in response to changing global conditions and emerging challenges. Staying informed about their ongoing activities and evolving roles is essential for anyone seeking to navigate the ever-changing world of international finance.

6.3 Emerging Markets and Development

The allure of emerging markets lies in their potential for rapid growth, offering investors the chance to capitalize on expanding economies and burgeoning consumer bases. But this potential comes with a unique set of risks, often intertwined with the very factors that drive their growth. Understanding these risks, and how to mitigate them, is crucial for successful investment in these dynamic landscapes. Political instability, for instance, can dramatically impact investment returns. A sudden shift in government policy, or a period of social unrest, can disrupt operations, devalue assets, and create an uncertain environment for businesses. Therefore, conducting thorough due diligence on the political landscape of a target market, including its history, current leadership, and potential for future instability, is a non-negotiable first step.

Navigating the regulatory environment presents another significant challenge. Emerging markets often lack the robust legal frameworks and transparent regulatory processes found in developed economies. This can lead to unexpected changes in regulations, bureaucratic hurdles, and even corruption, all of which can significantly hinder business operations and profitability. Investors must carefully assess the regulatory landscape of a target market, seeking expert local advice to understand the specific rules and regulations governing their investments. Building relationships with local officials and legal experts can provide valuable insights and help navigate potential regulatory challenges. This proactive approach can significantly reduce the risk of unforeseen complications and ensure smoother operations.

Currency fluctuations pose a constant threat to investments in emerging markets. Rapid and unpredictable changes in exchange rates can erode profits and significantly impact the value of assets. For example, a depreciation of the local currency against the investor's home currency can diminish the value of returns when repatriated. Employing hedging strategies, such as currency forwards or options, can mitigate this risk by locking in exchange rates and protecting against adverse currency movements. Diversifying investments across multiple emerging markets can also help to offset the impact of currency fluctuations in any single market.

Infrastructure limitations are another key consideration. Inadequate transportation networks, unreliable power grids, and limited access to technology can hinder business operations and increase costs. Before investing, it's essential to assess the quality and reliability of the infrastructure in the target market. This includes evaluating the transportation system, communication networks, and access to essential utilities. Understanding these limitations allows investors to factor in potential delays, disruptions, and increased operational costs. Furthermore, investing in companies that are actively addressing these infrastructure gaps can present attractive opportunities for long-term growth.

Social and environmental factors also play a crucial role. Emerging markets often face challenges related to poverty, inequality, and environmental degradation. These issues can impact business operations, create social unrest, and damage a company's reputation. Investors should prioritize companies that demonstrate a commitment to sustainable development and social responsibility. This includes assessing their environmental impact, labor practices, and community engagement. Investing in companies that prioritize these factors can not only mitigate risks but also contribute to positive social and environmental outcomes.

Market liquidity, or the ease with which assets can be bought or sold, can be significantly lower in emerging markets compared to developed markets. This can make it difficult to quickly exit an investment if market conditions deteriorate. Investors should carefully assess the liquidity of the target market and consider the potential challenges of selling assets in a downturn. Investing in more liquid assets, such as publicly traded stocks, can offer greater flexibility compared to illiquid assets like real estate. Furthermore, understanding the local trading practices and regulations is essential for navigating the market effectively.

Information asymmetry, where some market participants have access to more information than others, is often more pronounced in emerging markets. This can create an uneven playing field and expose investors to greater risks. Conducting thorough research, seeking independent analysis, and building relationships with local experts can help mitigate this risk. By accessing reliable information and developing a deep understanding of the market, investors can make more informed decisions and reduce their vulnerability to information asymmetry. Transparency and access to reliable data are vital for making sound investment choices.

Finally, the legal and judicial systems in emerging markets can be less developed and less predictable than those in developed economies. This can make it difficult to enforce contracts, protect intellectual property, and resolve disputes. Understanding the legal framework and seeking expert legal advice are crucial steps for mitigating this risk. Investors should also consider using arbitration clauses in contracts and structuring investments in a way that minimizes their exposure to legal uncertainties. Working with experienced legal counsel specializing in the target market can provide valuable guidance and protection.

Successfully navigating the complexities of emerging markets requires a long-term perspective, a deep understanding of the specific risks and opportunities, and a willingness to adapt to changing conditions. By conducting thorough due diligence, building strong relationships with local partners, and implementing appropriate risk mitigation strategies, investors can position themselves to capitalize on the immense potential of these dynamic markets. The rewards can be substantial for those who are prepared to navigate the challenges.

7 The Future of Finance

Finance stands on the precipice of transformative change. The convergence of technological advancements, evolving societal values, and shifting geopolitical landscapes is reshaping the very fabric of financial systems. Understanding these forces is crucial for navigating the complexities of the future financial world.

Decentralized finance (DeFi) is rapidly gaining traction, challenging traditional financial intermediaries. Peer-to-peer lending platforms, decentralized exchanges, and automated market makers are disrupting established models of banking, lending, and investment. This shift empowers individuals and reduces reliance on centralized institutions, fostering greater financial inclusion and potentially lowering transaction costs. However, the nascent nature of DeFi also presents unique challenges, including regulatory uncertainty and the potential for systemic risks. Careful consideration of these complexities is essential for harnessing the transformative potential of DeFi while mitigating its inherent vulnerabilities. Understanding the intricacies of smart contracts, blockchain governance, and decentralized autonomous organizations (DAOs) becomes paramount.

Biometric security systems, quantum computing, and advanced analytics are revolutionizing how financial institutions operate and interact with their customers. Biometric authentication offers enhanced security measures, safeguarding against fraud and identity theft. Quantum computing holds the potential to transform risk management and investment strategies through its unparalleled computational power, allowing for complex modeling and simulations. Advanced analytics, fueled by the explosion of data, enable personalized financial services, tailored investment advice, and more efficient fraud detection. Embracing these technological advancements requires a proactive approach to adaptation and a commitment to continuous learning.

The rise of sustainable finance and Environmental, Social, and Governance (ESG) investing reflects a growing awareness of the interconnectedness between financial systems and global sustainability. Investors are increasingly incorporating ESG factors into their decision-making, prioritizing companies committed to responsible environmental practices, social equity, and strong corporate governance. This shift is driving the development of new financial instruments, such as green bonds and social impact bonds, that channel capital towards projects with positive environmental and social outcomes. Understanding the nuances of ESG frameworks, impact measurement, and sustainable investment strategies becomes essential for navigating this evolving landscape.

Central banks worldwide are grappling with the implications of digital currencies and exploring the potential for Central Bank Digital Currencies (CBDCs). CBDCs offer the promise of increased financial inclusion, reduced transaction costs, and enhanced monetary policy effectiveness. However, they also raise concerns regarding privacy, security, and the potential for disrupting existing financial systems. The ongoing research and pilot programs exploring CBDCs represent a significant step towards shaping the future of money and payments. Keeping abreast of these developments and understanding the potential implications for monetary policy, financial stability, and the global financial architecture is crucial.

International cooperation and regulatory frameworks are undergoing a significant transformation to address the challenges of a rapidly globalizing financial landscape. The increasing interconnectedness of financial markets necessitates greater coordination among nations to prevent systemic risks and ensure financial stability. The rise of new financial technologies and the emergence of new players in the global financial system require innovative regulatory approaches that balance innovation with consumer protection. Active participation in shaping these global frameworks and engaging in constructive dialogue with international partners is essential for navigating the complexities of the future financial world. The future of finance is not a predetermined destination, but rather a dynamic process shaped by the interplay of technological advancements, societal values, and geopolitical forces. Embracing a mindset of continuous learning, adaptability, and proactive engagement is paramount for navigating this transformative era. By understanding the key trends shaping the future of finance, individuals and institutions can position themselves to thrive in a rapidly evolving financial landscape. This requires a deep understanding of the factors driving change, a willingness to embrace new technologies and approaches, and a commitment to fostering a more inclusive, sustainable, and resilient financial system. The future of finance demands a proactive approach to learning, adaptation, and collaboration. By embracing these principles, we can unlock the transformative potential of finance and build a more prosperous and equitable future for all. This requires a dedication to continuous learning, a willingness to adapt to new technologies and regulatory frameworks, and a proactive approach to shaping the future of finance through collaboration and innovation. This journey necessitates embracing uncertainty, fostering dialogue, and working together to build a more resilient and inclusive financial system that serves the needs of a rapidly changing world.

7.1 Technological Disruption in Finance

The financial landscape is in constant flux, a churning sea of innovation driven by relentless technological advancement. This creates both exciting opportunities and significant challenges for established players and newcomers alike. Understanding the forces at play is crucial for navigating this new terrain and capitalizing on the potential for growth and transformation. Forget the static models of the past; the future of finance is dynamic, interconnected, and increasingly digital. Consider the rise of fintech. These agile, tech-driven companies are disrupting traditional financial services by offering innovative solutions to age-old problems. Peer-to-peer lending platforms are bypassing traditional banks, connecting borrowers and lenders directly. Mobile payment systems are revolutionizing how we transact, making cash increasingly obsolete. Robo-advisors are providing personalized investment advice at a fraction of the cost of human advisors. These are just a few examples of how technology is reshaping the financial industry, forcing established institutions to adapt or risk being left behind.

This disruption isn't limited to individual services. The very infrastructure of finance is being reimagined. Blockchain technology, the foundation of cryptocurrencies, has the potential to revolutionize how we store and transfer value. Its decentralized and secure nature offers a compelling alternative to traditional centralized systems, promising greater transparency and efficiency. Smart contracts, self-executing agreements written in code, automate complex financial processes, reducing the need for intermediaries and streamlining transactions. These innovations are not merely incremental improvements; they represent a fundamental shift in how the financial system operates.

Navigating this rapidly changing environment requires a keen understanding of the underlying technological trends. One key trend is the increasing use of artificial intelligence and machine learning. These technologies are being applied to a wide range of financial tasks, from fraud detection and risk assessment to algorithmic trading and personalized financial advice. The ability to analyze vast amounts of data and identify patterns allows financial institutions to make more informed decisions, improve efficiency, and enhance customer experiences.

Another important trend is the growing importance of data security and privacy. As financial transactions become increasingly digital, the risk of cyberattacks and data breaches rises. Protecting sensitive financial information is paramount, and institutions must invest heavily in robust security measures to safeguard customer data and maintain trust. Regulations like GDPR and CCPA are further emphasizing the importance of data privacy, forcing companies to adopt more stringent data protection practices.

The rise of open banking is also transforming the financial landscape. Open banking allows third-party developers to access customer banking data through APIs, enabling the creation of innovative financial products and services. This fosters competition and empowers consumers with greater control over their financial data. It also creates opportunities for personalized financial management tools and customized financial solutions tailored to individual needs.

Furthermore, the increasing convergence of finance and technology is blurring the lines between traditional financial institutions and tech companies. Tech giants are entering the financial services market, leveraging their vast user bases and technological expertise to offer innovative financial products. This competition is driving innovation and forcing traditional financial institutions to embrace digital transformation to remain competitive.

The implications of these technological disruptions are far-reaching. They are changing the way we interact with financial institutions, how businesses manage their finances, and how regulators oversee the financial system. For consumers, this means greater access to financial services, more personalized experiences, and potentially lower costs. For businesses, it means improved efficiency, greater transparency, and new opportunities for growth. For regulators, it means adapting existing regulations and developing new frameworks to address the unique challenges posed by these technological innovations.

However, these disruptions also present challenges. The rapid pace of change can be overwhelming, and keeping up with the latest technologies can be difficult. There is also the

risk of unintended consequences, such as increased inequality, job displacement, and systemic risks. Addressing these challenges requires a collaborative approach involving industry players, regulators, and policymakers.
Adapting to this new era of finance requires a willingness to embrace change, a commitment to continuous learning, and a proactive approach to innovation. Those who can navigate this complex landscape and harness the power of technology will be well-positioned to thrive in the future of finance. The future is not something to be feared, but rather an opportunity to be seized. By understanding the forces driving technological disruption, we can shape a financial system that is more efficient, inclusive, and resilient. The journey is just beginning, and the possibilities are endless.

7.2 Cryptocurrencies and Blockchain

The allure of cryptocurrencies stems from their decentralized nature, operating outside the control of traditional financial institutions. This independence offers a potential shield against inflation and economic instability, as well as faster and cheaper transactions across borders. However, this new financial landscape comes with its own set of complexities and risks that warrant careful consideration. Understanding the underlying technology, blockchain, is crucial for navigating this evolving space.

Blockchain, the foundational technology behind most cryptocurrencies, functions as a distributed, immutable ledger. Imagine a digital record-keeping system, shared among a vast network of computers. Every transaction is grouped into a "block," cryptographically secured and linked to the preceding block, forming a chain. This chronological chain of records ensures transparency and tamper-proof security. It is this decentralized and secure nature of blockchain that lends credence and functionality to cryptocurrencies.

Delving deeper into cryptocurrencies, it's important to differentiate between various types. Bitcoin, the first and most well-known cryptocurrency, serves primarily as a store of value, similar to digital gold. Ethereum, on the other hand, provides a platform for decentralized applications (dApps) and smart contracts, enabling a wide array of functionalities beyond simple transactions. Other cryptocurrencies cater to specific niches, such as privacy-focused coins like Monero or those designed for supply chain management. Understanding the specific purpose and underlying technology of each cryptocurrency is essential for making informed investment decisions.

Before venturing into the world of cryptocurrency investment, it's paramount to establish a clear investment strategy. Define your financial goals, risk tolerance, and time horizon. Are you looking for short-term gains or long-term growth? How much volatility are you comfortable with? Diversification is key, spreading your investment across different cryptocurrencies and asset classes to mitigate risk. Thoroughly research each cryptocurrency, understanding its underlying technology, market capitalization, and future potential. Avoid investing based on hype or speculation, and rely on sound fundamental analysis.

Navigating the cryptocurrency market requires understanding the various exchanges and platforms available. Centralized exchanges, similar to traditional stock exchanges, provide a platform for buying, selling, and trading cryptocurrencies. Decentralized exchanges, on the other hand, offer greater control over your assets and enhanced privacy. Choose a reputable exchange with robust security measures, low fees, and a user-friendly interface. Ensure the exchange supports the specific cryptocurrencies you wish to trade. Familiarize yourself with the platform's features and functionalities before making any transactions.

Security is paramount in the cryptocurrency space. Given the decentralized nature of these assets, securing your private keys is crucial. These keys are essentially your digital signature, granting access to your cryptocurrency holdings. Store your private keys offline, in a hardware wallet or on a secure physical medium. Never share your private keys with anyone. Be wary of phishing scams and fraudulent schemes that attempt to steal your credentials. Exercise caution when interacting with unfamiliar websites or individuals online.

Beyond individual investment, the potential of blockchain extends far beyond cryptocurrencies. Its distributed and secure nature has transformative implications across various industries. Supply chain management can benefit from increased transparency and traceability, enabling efficient tracking of goods and materials. Healthcare can leverage blockchain for secure storage and sharing of patient data. Voting systems can be enhanced with greater transparency and security, ensuring the integrity of elections. The applications of blockchain are vast and continue to evolve, shaping the future of various sectors.

As with any emerging technology, regulatory landscapes surrounding cryptocurrencies are still developing. Governments worldwide are grappling with how to regulate this new asset class, balancing innovation with consumer protection. Stay informed about regulatory developments in your jurisdiction and comply with all applicable laws and regulations. Be aware that regulations can impact the price and availability of cryptocurrencies. Engage with reputable sources of information to stay abreast of the evolving regulatory environment.

Tax implications of cryptocurrency transactions can be complex and vary depending on your jurisdiction. Consult with a qualified tax advisor to understand the tax implications of buying, selling, and holding cryptocurrencies. Keep meticulous records of all your transactions, including dates, amounts, and exchange rates. Be prepared to report your cryptocurrency holdings and transactions to the relevant tax authorities. Understanding the tax implications is crucial for avoiding penalties and complying with regulations.

The future of cryptocurrencies and blockchain remains uncertain, yet full of potential. As the technology matures and adoption increases, we can expect further innovation and integration into various aspects of our lives. Staying informed, conducting thorough research, and exercising caution are crucial for navigating this dynamic landscape. By understanding the underlying technology, managing risks effectively, and embracing the potential of blockchain, you can participate in this exciting new frontier of finance and technology. Remember that continuous learning and adaptation are essential for success in the ever-evolving world of cryptocurrencies and blockchain.

7.3 Sustainable Finance and ESG Investing

The world of finance is changing. No longer are profits the sole measure of success. Investors are increasingly recognizing the interconnectedness of financial performance with environmental, social, and governance (ESG) factors. This shift marks a significant evolution in how we assess value, demanding a deeper understanding of the long-term implications of investment decisions. Sustainable finance aims to channel capital towards activities that contribute to a more sustainable future, integrating ESG considerations into investment analysis and decision-making processes. This isn't simply a trend; it's a fundamental reshaping of the financial landscape, offering both opportunities and challenges for investors.

One of the key drivers behind this shift is the growing awareness of environmental risks. Climate change, resource depletion, and pollution pose substantial threats to businesses and the global economy. Companies with poor environmental practices face increasing scrutiny from regulators, consumers, and investors. They might encounter higher operating costs due to resource scarcity, fines for non-compliance, and reputational damage. Conversely, companies that prioritize sustainability are better positioned to navigate these challenges, potentially gaining a competitive advantage and attracting environmentally conscious investors. This dynamic is pushing investors to evaluate environmental risks and opportunities more rigorously, leading to greater demand for sustainable investment options.

Social factors are equally crucial in assessing long-term value. These include a company's relationships with its employees, customers, suppliers, and the communities in which it operates. Factors like fair labor practices, product safety, and community engagement are no longer peripheral concerns but integral to a company's overall performance. Companies with strong social performance often benefit from improved employee morale and productivity, enhanced brand reputation, and stronger stakeholder relationships. Ignoring social factors can lead to reputational damage, consumer boycotts, and legal challenges, all of which can significantly impact a company's bottom line. This underscores the importance of integrating social considerations into investment decisions.

Governance refers to the internal structures and processes by which a company is managed and overseen. This includes aspects such as board composition, executive compensation, and shareholder rights. Strong corporate governance promotes transparency, accountability, and ethical decision-making. Companies with robust governance structures are less likely to experience scandals, fraud, and mismanagement, which can erode shareholder value. Conversely, weak governance can lead to financial losses, regulatory intervention, and damage to investor confidence. Therefore, evaluating governance practices is essential for making informed investment choices.

ESG investing takes various forms, catering to different investment philosophies and risk appetites. One approach is negative screening, which involves excluding companies involved in controversial activities, such as tobacco production, weapons manufacturing, or fossil fuel extraction. Another approach is positive screening, which focuses on investing in companies with strong ESG performance. This involves identifying companies that demonstrate leadership in areas such as environmental sustainability, social responsibility, and corporate governance. Impact investing goes a step further, aiming to generate measurable social or environmental impact alongside financial returns. This might involve investing in renewable energy projects, affordable housing initiatives, or companies providing access to essential services in underserved communities.

Integrating ESG factors into investment analysis requires a comprehensive approach. Traditional financial metrics, such as revenue, earnings, and cash flow, remain important. However, these metrics need to be supplemented with ESG data and analysis. This involves assessing a company's environmental footprint, social impact, and governance practices. Investors can utilize various resources, including ESG ratings agencies, sustainability reports, and third-party research, to gather information and evaluate a company's ESG performance.

The growing availability of ESG data and tools is facilitating the integration of sustainability into investment decisions. ESG ratings agencies provide assessments of companies' ESG performance, allowing investors to compare and contrast different investments. Sustainability reports, published by companies themselves, offer insights into their ESG strategies and initiatives. Furthermore, specialized software and data platforms are emerging, enabling investors to analyze and track ESG data more efficiently. These resources empower investors to make more informed decisions and hold companies accountable for their sustainability performance.

Sustainable finance is not without its challenges. One key challenge is the lack of standardized ESG reporting. Different companies use different metrics and methodologies to report on their ESG performance, making it difficult to compare apples to apples. This lack of standardization can create confusion and hinder effective decision-making. Another challenge is the potential for "greenwashing," where companies exaggerate their sustainability efforts to attract investors. It is essential for investors to critically evaluate ESG claims and ensure that companies are genuinely committed to sustainability.

Despite these challenges, the momentum behind sustainable finance is undeniable. The increasing awareness of ESG issues, coupled with the growing demand for sustainable investment options, is driving significant change in the financial industry. Regulators are also playing a role, introducing policies and regulations to promote sustainable finance and enhance transparency. These developments are creating a more favorable environment for ESG investing and paving the way for a more sustainable future.

Ultimately, sustainable finance is about aligning financial decisions with long-term value creation. By considering environmental, social, and governance factors, investors can identify companies that are better positioned for long-term success and contribute to a more sustainable world. This shift towards sustainable investing represents a profound transformation of the financial landscape, offering both opportunities and responsibilities for investors, companies, and society as a whole. As the world grapples with pressing environmental and social challenges, sustainable finance offers a path towards a more equitable and resilient future.

7.4 The Evolving Role of Central Banks

The gold standard, a system where currencies were pegged to the value of gold, represented a simpler era for central banking. Its inherent limitations, like the constraint on money supply growth and vulnerability to gold discoveries, eventually led to its demise. This paved the way for a more active role for central banks, evolving from mere custodians of gold reserves to managers of monetary policy. Their mandate shifted towards maintaining price stability, promoting full employment, and ensuring the smooth functioning of financial systems. This transition wasn't immediate but rather a gradual process, punctuated by economic crises and shifting global dynamics.

The Bretton Woods system, established after World War II, marked a significant step in this evolution. It pegged currencies to the US dollar, which in turn was linked to gold. This system provided a degree of stability, facilitating post-war reconstruction and international trade. However, its inherent dependence on the US economy and the growing divergence between the dollar's value and gold reserves eventually led to its collapse in the early 1970s. This marked the beginning of the era of floating exchange rates, a system where currency values are determined by market forces, further increasing the complexity of central banking.

With the end of Bretton Woods, central banks gained greater autonomy in managing their monetary policies. Inflation targeting emerged as a dominant framework, with central banks setting explicit inflation targets and using interest rate adjustments as their primary tool to achieve these objectives. This approach demanded sophisticated economic modeling and forecasting capabilities. The need for transparency and accountability also grew, as central banks sought to build credibility and manage public expectations about future inflation and economic growth. Communication became a key element of monetary policy, with central bankers using public statements and reports to influence market perceptions and guide economic activity.

The late 20th and early 21st centuries witnessed a period of relative economic stability, often referred to as the "Great Moderation." This period was characterized by low and stable inflation, sustained economic growth, and reduced volatility in financial markets. Many attributed this success to the effectiveness of inflation targeting and the improved management of monetary policy by central banks. However, this period of calm was punctuated by occasional financial crises, underscoring the ongoing challenges and evolving nature of central banking.

The 2008 global financial crisis marked a turning point. It exposed vulnerabilities in the financial system and challenged conventional monetary policy tools. Central banks responded with unprecedented measures, including quantitative easing (QE), a process of injecting liquidity into the economy by purchasing assets like government bonds. This unconventional approach aimed to lower long-term interest rates and stimulate lending and investment when traditional interest rate cuts were no longer effective. The effectiveness of QE and its long-term consequences remain subjects of ongoing debate and research.

The subsequent years saw continued experimentation with unconventional monetary policy tools, including negative interest rates and forward guidance. These policies aimed to address persistent economic weakness and deflationary pressures in some advanced economies. However, they also raised concerns about their potential side effects, including distortions in financial markets and the erosion of bank profitability. Central banks also began to grapple with the implications of technological advancements, such as the rise of cryptocurrencies and the increasing digitalization of finance.

The evolving landscape of finance presented new challenges to central banks. The interconnectedness of global financial markets amplified the impact of shocks and crises, requiring greater international cooperation and coordination among central banks. The emergence of new financial instruments and technologies, like decentralized finance (DeFi), posed regulatory challenges and raised questions about the future of money and payments. Central banks began exploring the potential of central bank digital currencies (CBDCs) as a means to enhance monetary policy effectiveness and maintain their relevance in the evolving digital economy.

Climate change emerged as another significant factor influencing central bank mandates. The increasing frequency and severity of climate-related events posed systemic risks to financial stability. Central banks began to incorporate climate change considerations into their supervisory and regulatory frameworks, promoting sustainable finance and assessing the potential impact of climate change on the economy and financial system. The integration of climate change into monetary policy frameworks is an ongoing process, with many complexities and challenges to overcome.

The future role of central banks is likely to be shaped by several key trends. These include the ongoing digitalization of finance, the growing importance of sustainability and climate change, and the increasing complexity of global economic and financial interdependencies. Central banks will need to adapt and innovate to remain effective in this evolving landscape. This includes developing new tools and frameworks to address emerging challenges, strengthening international cooperation, and enhancing transparency and communication with the public. The evolution of central banking is a continuous journey, marked by both successes and challenges, reflecting the dynamic nature of the global economy and financial system. Their ability to navigate these complexities will be crucial for maintaining stability and promoting sustainable economic growth in the years to come. The ongoing dialogue between central banks, policymakers, academics, and the public will be essential to shaping the future of monetary policy and ensuring its effectiveness in serving the public interest.

7.5 The Future of Global Economic Governance

The global economic landscape is shifting. Power dynamics are evolving, and the institutions designed to manage international economic cooperation are facing unprecedented challenges. These challenges stem from a variety of sources: the rise of new economic powers, the increasing interconnectedness of global markets, and the emergence of complex transnational issues like climate change and cybersecurity. Adapting to these evolving realities requires a critical examination of existing governance structures and a willingness to embrace innovative solutions. The future of global economic governance hinges on our ability to foster greater inclusivity, transparency, and responsiveness within the international system.

One of the most pressing issues facing global economic governance is the need for reform within international financial institutions. The Bretton Woods institutions, established in the aftermath of World War II, have played a crucial role in promoting global economic stability and development. However, their legitimacy and effectiveness are increasingly being questioned, particularly by developing countries who feel their voices are not adequately represented. Reforming these institutions to better reflect the current global economic order, including greater representation for emerging economies, is essential for ensuring their continued relevance and legitimacy. This includes revising voting rights, quota shares, and leadership selection processes to be more inclusive and representative of the changing global economic landscape.

Beyond institutional reform, the future of global economic governance also depends on strengthening international cooperation on a range of critical issues. Climate change, for instance, poses a significant threat to global economic stability and requires a coordinated international response. Developing and implementing effective mechanisms for carbon pricing, investing in renewable energy technologies, and promoting sustainable development practices are crucial for mitigating the economic risks associated with climate change. Similarly, addressing the growing challenges posed by cybersecurity requires international cooperation on issues such as data protection, cross-border data flows, and the development of common standards and norms.

The rise of regional economic agreements and blocs presents both opportunities and challenges for global economic governance. While regional agreements can foster closer economic ties and promote regional integration, they can also potentially undermine multilateralism and fragment the global trading system. Striking a balance between regionalism and multilateralism is crucial for ensuring a stable and open global economy. This involves working to ensure that regional agreements are consistent with broader multilateral rules and principles, and that they contribute to, rather than detract from, global economic cooperation. Promoting dialogue and coordination between regional and multilateral institutions is also essential.

The increasing interconnectedness of global markets has also highlighted the need for greater regulatory coherence. Divergent regulatory frameworks across different jurisdictions can create inefficiencies, increase compliance costs for businesses, and hinder cross-border trade and investment. Working towards greater regulatory harmonization and convergence, particularly in areas such as financial regulation, trade policy, and environmental protection, can facilitate greater cross-border economic activity and promote a more level playing field for businesses operating globally. This could involve the development of international standards and best practices, as well as enhanced information sharing and regulatory cooperation between countries.

Another key aspect of the future of global economic governance is the need to enhance transparency and accountability. Decisions made within international institutions often lack transparency, making it difficult for stakeholders to understand the rationale behind these decisions and hold decision-makers accountable. Increasing transparency in decision-making processes, including greater public access to information and more inclusive consultations with civil society organizations and other stakeholders, can enhance the legitimacy and effectiveness of global economic governance. This could involve establishing clear guidelines for transparency and accountability within international institutions, as well as mechanisms for monitoring and evaluating their performance.

Furthermore, the future of global economic governance requires addressing the growing gap between the rich and the poor. Inequality, both within and between countries, poses a significant threat to global economic stability and social cohesion. Promoting inclusive growth, ensuring equitable access to opportunities, and investing in social safety nets are essential for reducing inequality and fostering sustainable development. This requires a multi-faceted approach that includes policies aimed at promoting job creation, improving access to education and healthcare, and strengthening social protection systems.

Technological advancements are also transforming the global economic landscape and presenting new challenges for governance. The rapid development and deployment of new technologies, such as artificial intelligence and blockchain, have the potential to disrupt existing industries, create new economic opportunities, and reshape global value chains. Developing appropriate regulatory frameworks for these emerging technologies is essential for ensuring that they are used responsibly and for the benefit of all. This includes addressing issues such as data privacy, cybersecurity, and the ethical implications of artificial intelligence.

Finally, fostering greater public trust in global economic governance is crucial for its long-term sustainability. Public skepticism towards globalization and international institutions has grown in recent years, fueled by concerns about job losses, income inequality, and the perceived erosion of national sovereignty. Building public trust requires demonstrating the tangible benefits of international cooperation, ensuring that the voices of all stakeholders are heard, and promoting greater transparency and accountability in decision-making processes. This involves engaging in open and honest dialogue with the public, addressing their concerns, and showcasing the positive impacts of global economic cooperation. The future of global economic governance depends on our collective ability to adapt to these evolving challenges and build a more inclusive, resilient, and sustainable global economy.

www.ingramcontent.com/pod-product-compliance
Lightning Source LLC
LaVergne TN
LVHW022219200926
848481LV00006B/2028
* 9 7 9 8 3 4 8 3 1 6 6 4 8 *